777

PURPOSE AND TRUTH OVER RESISTANCE

Staying Aligned with God's Path

BARBANNE BAINER

BALBOA
PRESS
A DIVISION OF HAY HOUSE

Balboa Press books may be ordered through booksellers or by contacting:

Balboa Press
A Division of Hay House
1663 Liberty Drive
Bloomington, IN 47403
www.balboapress.com
1 (877) 407-4847

Because of the dynamic nature of the Internet, any web addresses or links contained in this book may have changed since publication and may no longer be valid. The views expressed in this work are solely those of the author and do not necessarily reflect the views of the publisher, and the publisher hereby disclaims any responsibility for them.

The author of this book does not dispense medical advice or prescribe the use of any technique as a form of treatment for physical, emotional, or medical problems without the advice of a physician, either directly or indirectly. The intent of the author is only to offer information of a general nature to help you in your quest for emotional and spiritual well-being. In the event you use any of the information in this book for yourself, which is your constitutional right, the author and the publisher assume no responsibility for your actions.

Any people depicted in stock imagery provided by Thinkstock are models,
and such images are being used for illustrative purposes only.
Certain stock imagery © Thinkstock.

Print information available on the last page.

ISBN: 978-1-5043-5762-3 (sc)
ISBN: 978-1-5043-5763-0 (e)

Library of Congress Control Number: 2016907921

Balboa Press rev. date: 05/26/2016

Thank you to everyone who has been a part of my journey.
You know who you are.

CONTENTS

INTRODUCTION

When I was completing a previous manuscript, I connected to my Spiritual Destiny and realized that other books were to follow. The vibration of this new material felt higher than what I had received before. I naturally wanted to know the title and what it would contain. I thought that it might be about Archangel Gabriel, but I was still trying to access the information. Because I had gone through the same process with my earlier writing, I recognized that there were blocks to my receiving and hearing the communications. Sometimes it is because my mind can't wrap itself around the subject matter. This time I felt a very strong outdated vow or contract. When my Higher Guidance directed me to hold a pen on a pad of paper, I thought that this might be the way the writing would come through, but instead I saw myself in a past life trying to write some of this same information.

I was a young monk in Nepal, who had been sent to a mountain cave to obtain channeled knowledge and bring it back. I was aware that there was one other person in the cave with me doing the same meditation for enlightenment. I realized that the elders had already sent me back because they did not like or want a written record of what I had clearly received. Some time later I returned to them with the same messages and was eventually killed by my peers at the elders' direction. The writing was destroyed.

If that wasn't enough reason for not bringing through the information in my current lifetime, there were even more blocks: a very strong vow or contract between lifetimes, which prevented me from continuing the writing until that block was cleared, as well as several more blocks contained within my Soul Destiny. I pushed through one step at a time, not knowing what to expect or what words would come. Each word brought an energy that opened my mind to receive the next. This is not an easy journey.

The book's title "777" is the Subconscious error code correction that enables you to step out of the fog of not knowing what to do. You allow your purpose and truth to override your resistance so that you can accomplish all you entered into this lifetime to achieve. Try it the next time you are unsure of what to do. Say "777" or "I allow my purpose to outweigh my resistance."

Part 1 brings new concepts to both students and teachers of the Divine's training academy, to which we are all plugged in. This is our ability to connect up higher in order to relay thoughts and lessons from God/Source through the eyes of the Divine rather than our own. It begins with a brief overview of my own journey followed by detailed instructions for navigating the barriers of your ego and subconscious mind, techniques for building your intuition, and original key phrases for allowing your growth to expand beyond what you believe you can accomplish. Teachers will find instructions for guiding intuitives and mediums who want to work on investigative cases. Combining my experience in law enforcement with advanced-level instruction in the intuitive arts has brought new ideas and structure to teaching intuition and psychic skills.

Part 2 is channeled writing that came through during the meditation and healing work I do every day. The most important part of a channeled message is what it is for the receiver. Every message will cause a different reaction, resonance, and truth for each person. Messages from the Divine can touch multiple dimensions and ways of thinking as well as transfer Divine intervention and healing. A channel is often unaware of what result the words will bring. The majority of this section is channeled from Jesus and the *Bible* with messages from Archangels Metatron and Gabriel. I hope you enjoy reading these words as much as I did writing them.

PART 1

I spent many years of my life without love, support, encouragement, or protection. My young, alcoholic mother left me behind as she went to a local bar, left my father and me for over a year without contacting us, and then brought a stepfather into my life, who was an alcoholic and pedophile. I knew I wanted more than this for myself and my future.

I was in middle school when a local ten-year-old boy was sexually assaulted, stabbed to death, and left in a creek bed by a fourteen-year-old acquaintance of one of my friends. Being so close to a crime makes you feel unsafe. I wanted to help others and hopefully prevent crimes like these from happening. I never knew that this would be one of the changing moments in my life.

As I look back at the opportunities that opened up for me, I see the Divine guidance that was there even when I was not aware of it. When I was seventeen, I moved out of my family home and rented an apartment with my best friend Barb. I was hired as a police cadet community service officer. From ages seventeen to twenty-one, I worked in many areas of the police agency: animal control, records, and 9-1-1 dispatch. At twenty-one, I passed the police exam on the first try and was hired as an officer. I quickly moved through the ranks, working in DARE/crime prevention, patrol, evidence, juvenile, and as a field training officer. I was promoted to Sergeant over two other officers with longer tenure, making me the first female supervisor in that Chicago suburb. But after fifteen years in law enforcement, I retired early because the department was not supportive of my second pregnancy. Forced to make a decision between family and work, I chose family.

I have been married twice and have three children. I can now say that after this entire journey of self-growth and healing I am happy. I have worked through all that you can imagine to find my own self-worth and to trust in others and the Universe. I have not been alone. I am thankful that I have always had the support of my father. My husband is the light in my world, along with my children and my connection to God.

I have not always known that I was connecting with a higher power even though I did hear the warnings of the Universe on several occasions. A voice told my teenage self to put on my seatbelt right before a car in which I was a passenger rolled over. On my police job, I always seemed to have a sense of what would happen next. I could tell when someone was going to run or was being deceptive. I knew when I needed to check into something further or be ready to act. I called this being street smart and having good common sense, but I can see now it was a bit more than that. On one occasion I was giving CPR to an unresponsive elderly man, and I heard him tell me that it was his time and I could stop. I remember thinking that I had seen many people do CPR and bring people back...I did not bring him back. I am sure many other people have the Divine connecting to them and just think it is normal for everyone.

After retiring from the police department, I started a custom glass tile business. I worked out of my garage making kiln-formed glass for local kitchen/bath designers and custom tile shops. I received orders from some high-end businesses in my area, and one of them even displayed my work at Chicago's Merchandise Mart. But eventually the collapse of the housing market ended the tile business.

Just after the housing market failed, my friend Barb died unexpectedly from natural causes. Two days later, a close family member of one of my previous police supervisors was reported missing under suspicious circumstances. I could feel both of them in spirit form. This was when I had confirmation that there was something more than what I had been aware of before. My world was flooded with information coming through very lucid dreams and sensory vibrations. I did not have a background of mediumship or psychic ability and had much to learn. I started connecting with Spirit Guides through dreams and visions, not even knowing what I was experiencing.

I searched out places where other psychics were interested in missing persons cases and began the process of spiritual enlightenment. I connected with a local mediumship group and made lifelong friends for my journey. I had some people take advantage of my gifts and information until I realized that everyone is human, even if they are aware of the fact that there is more beyond just us.

My most effective learning began when I realized that no one other than my own connection with God/Source and my Higher Guidance was going to teach me what I needed to know. So many people teaching, but not at the level I was at. They were explaining things through their own filters and biases, which was of little help for me.

I have enjoyed the many friends I have met along the way. Some of them moved on when I started teaching myself, but that is to be expected. Energy moves and is not meant to be captured in a box for storage. Not everyone's path is the same one to be traveled together.

Connecting with Spirit

How can I connect with my Higher Self?

For the longest time I could not hear the name of my Higher Self, as it was not in my mindset or paradigm. It did not even make sense that God would talk directly to me. It does now, and I regularly connect people to that reality through personal and group sessions. When I could speak with my Spirit Guides and realized that I was talking to God/Source and that my Higher Self was an Archangel named Metatron, understanding my journey became easier. Not that telling people that the higher part of me is a heavenly scribe, Director of Karma, and supporter of higher realms is easy. It was not something I had to do until now. I was also given some of my past life identities, several recognizable, but luckily I do not need to draw attention to them. I do need to share enough of my personal experience with you to open your paradigm to these possibilities.

When you want to know more about your Higher Self, ask to receive information only at the highest God/Source connection. A specific energy might come into your mind or senses. Be open. Yes, some humans can be an Archangel, Ascended Master, or Saint at the Higher Self or Soul level. Once I broke through that paradigm, I learned that many other people are here grounding the energy of their Higher Self for the same purpose. So many Souls are here to help bring the Earth and other realms to a higher vibration or standing, through knowledge and change. I also found out that a Soul can have more than one incarnation at a time. I asked how many of us connected to my Higher Self, Metatron, there were on Earth at that time and was told twenty-three in physical body. When I asked at the time of this writing, it was twenty-seven. Souls are being born and transitioning back to spirit all the time. I also learned that some Higher Selves are specifically used to help guide humans in spirit form, and some will incarnate only on rare occasions.

Not everyone's Higher Self is an ascended Master, Saint, or Archangel. Many people are here from different realms. There are light workers from places other than this world: Alien, ET, Light Beings, Star People, Star Children, Elementals, and other Manifesting Beings of Light. The interconnectedness of this realm crosses paths with all other realms, giving us all the common cause of healing humanity one being at a time.

There are also people here to experience love from beginning phases as a human being. Much of their time has been spent working up to higher vibrations from the human perspective, generation after generation. It does not mean anyone is more important than the rest, just the realization that we are all here for varying reasons, missions, and vibrations of existence.

The Universe and beyond can be viewed as a body with areas of imbalance, like places of illness, needing to be brought into balance to effectively keep the system running. All beings are here to help with the same purpose. All have worth and interconnectedness, just like everyone on Earth has an interconnectedness and responsibility to one another.

The Universal Light Source has a special view of what you can bring to the healing and reprogramming of this realm. You may have had a hard life in this incarnation, but you will feel that underlying communication from who you are as a Soul leading you in an important direction. Some will get to fulfill their mission in this lifetime, while some will have barriers of the human mind that hold them back.

For those who are used to being in light form, the experience of being human is not easy. So many people come to me who are completely unhappy with the human body and this Earthly realm. They claim to not fit in or be comfortable in their own skin. They feel very abandoned or separate from the other people here in physical form. They long to be back in spirit form, and the whole physical process is too much for them to handle. When I connect to their Higher Self, I often find that they volunteered to come here for a specific purpose. As they reconnect with their higher true form and understand the bigger picture of why they are here, some of them feel more at peace. Just connecting with Source will allow you to feel a common interconnectedness with all things, even those you don't agree with.

Do I need to know the names of my Spirit Guides?

I never really worried about knowing the names of my Spirit Guides. It was five years of working with them before I felt prompted to know their names. I remember asking my Higher Self if I should have the names and being told no. However, at some point I felt encouraged by God/Source to retrieve the names.

This is one of the disagreements I have had with my Higher Self. Do not assume your Higher Self knows more than you. Always connect to the highest Source and have all your directing and growth start from there. In this case I asked my Higher Self why I shouldn't know and was told that it might make me have a large Ego mind. I asked, as directed by Source, if we have ever had too much Ego with that type of information and was told, "No."

Eventually I was given a list of twenty of my Spirit Guides' names. On it were many Ascended Masters, Archangels, Goddesses, and so on. Once I was given the names, I threw the paper out and continued my journey as I had before, Divinely guided and protected as guaranteed by my Soul Destiny and truth.

Do you need to know the names of your Spirit Guides? No, you do not. You always want guidance that brings you safely to the next and higher level with the least amount of difficulty and stress. Spend a few minutes in your daily meditation asking to connect to your Guides, your Higher Self, and Source so that you can start being able to tell the differences in the energetic voices and energy signatures of your Divine guidance and plan. If you feel something is off or not aligned, ask Source every once in a while if you have the highest Guides possible at this time in your journey.

What can I do to hear my Higher Guidance more clearly?

<u>Clearing Emotions</u>

When I first opened up to Spirit, I had a long list of imbalances and fears that I was still holding. As soon as I could hear my Higher Guidance, I was directed to get myself to the point where I could forgive those who had hurt me most in my life. I started with the person that I had the hardest time forgiving. I can remember having long talks with God on this issue and becoming convinced that not forgiving was holding me back. It locked up my heart. With a partially open heart, information could only come in sporadically. Sporadically was not good enough because I knew I needed clear answers and guidance for my gift and Soul Destiny. I spent hours of crying and releasing old hurts from my Soul and truth until I was told that I had lifted from me what I needed to.

At that point I was asked to send healing to the abuser. It took close to two weeks for me to realize that putting off this faith-based energy healing wasn't doing me any good. I sent the healing and could feel how it changed everything. It completely separated it from me, my energy field, and my Soul all at once. Any outdated vows or circumstances that keep your energy in unforgiveness will block clear connections every time, so forgive all of those who have harmed or hurt you, until no more remain. They will still need to deal with their own Karma.

The second part of forgiveness is to release any guilt, anger, hatred, jealousy, or greed that you are holding. Each one of these emotions blocks your connection to Source. These are considered Free Will choices and often cause imbalance in the physical body. When you forgive others, you have to remember that forgiving yourself will be an even more important battle. I energetically feel those harmful emotions being held in these parts of the body:

Greed – furthermost right side of body at the waist
Jealousy – furthermost left side of body at the waist
Envy – left side of the body, two inches right of Jealousy
Guilt – just right of Heart Chakra
Anger and Hatred – left side of Heart Chakra (place the Soul body is seated in the physical body)

How much you hold in any of these areas will affect your clear connection to the Divine. They will still be watching over you, but you will not feel or hear direct guidance since any of these areas are enough to strongly block the voice of the Divine. If you never forgive your ex-boyfriend, ex-girlfriend, ex-spouse, friend, family member, co-worker, neighbor, stranger, and so on, you will never have a clear connection with God/Source. A clear conversation can only be had without these mindsets and emotions. Forgive all and create a new paradigm. Please connect with a licensed therapist when doing this becomes emotional or difficult. I did. Certain things require help, so get help when you need it. Some may say letting go is not easy, but yes it is. When you no longer have a purpose for holding on to it, it is that easy. Decide to do it, and then do it.

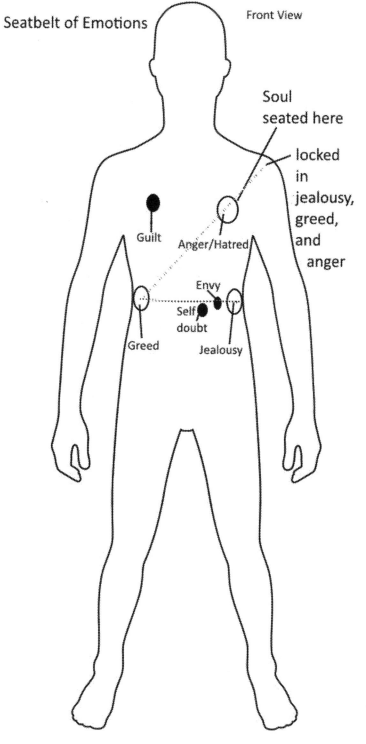

Seatbelt of Emotions

Front View

Soul
seated here

locked
in
jealousy,
greed,
and
anger

Guilt

Anger/Hatred

Envy

Self
doubt

Greed

Jealousy

Releasing Fears

Your fears are another area that affects how clear your connection is. Early in my clearing process, I was guided to address my fears. This is my list in order of severity: fear of death; fear of not completing this life's mission; spiders; scary movies; and abandonment.

We started with the fear of spiders, which I still have now, but the severity has decreased. Spirit had me hold a pendulum and watch it rotate counterclockwise to remove or disconnect the fear. I would induce the fear by thinking about spiders and then allow the energy to be lifted while holding the pendulum, which will swing counterclockwise on its own when energy is being removed. During the time period that I was getting the counterclockwise swing while doing this exercise, some past lifetimes with spiders were revealed through dreams and visions.

My initial reaction to seeing a crawling spider had always been to scream, but after a few sessions using this method, I was able to stay centered even though I did not care for the idea of a spider crawling near me. The next time I saw a spider, I used the pendulum to pull out that higher level of fear to allow me to get closer to it. After the pendulum swings counterclockwise until the fear energy has been pulled out, it will reverse and swing clockwise, indicating sending or filling up with positive energy. When the pendulum stops, you are finished.

This process will continue even when you are not holding the pendulum. In the event a pendulum is not a viable option, just visualize or think about energy being removed or lifted from you. Breathe and stay centered as much as you can while allowing yourself to lower your instinct, which means lowering the level of fear you have about the particular perceived threat or challenge. You will sometimes retain a level of fear to keep you safe. The programmed, ideal fear safety level will remain for whatever the issue is: heights, needing to act, crimes, allergies, or common threats. In this lifetime I have an allergic reaction (hives and fever) to spider bites, so I still have an alert at times for spider awareness.

The way that Spirit helped me to release the fear of death was not what I would have guessed, but it made sense. My Higher Guidance had me sit through my passing for this lifetime. I sat quietly with my eyes closed, did breathing, and allowed the information to come in. I knew that I was in my eighties and that I was holding my husband's hand. I was feeling peaceful, and I left my Earthly body, happy and at peace. It was without pain or fear, and I was not alone. After that experience, I no longer could be afraid because I had faced my fear, gotten complete information, and moved forward.

In order to clear the scary movies fear, my Guides had me stay on a television channel showing graphic images that bothered me and brought up my fear. Two men were using large machetes to chop off zombie-type creatures' heads. I used the pendulum swinging counterclockwise method for this one. I think it took three episodes of this show to completely clear the fear. It went from being scary, to disgusting, to ridiculously funny and entertaining. This became my favorite show to watch. I'm sure some of you enjoy this show, too.

Shortly after removing this fear, my Higher Guidance needed me to be able to knowingly allow my Soul to leave my body. I had no idea why this was necessary, but my Guides said that I needed the awareness and that they would stay close. The idea seemed scary at the time, so I used the pendulum technique until I was just outside of my body. It was a new feeling and experience, but it was not scary. The timing of releasing this fear allowed me to help a client the following day, who had recently lost her husband due to a sudden heart attack. I could feel part of her Soul had left her body with this loss. I could hear my Guides say to assist her in properly seating the Soul back into her body. I would not have had this awareness if I had not had my own experience of what the Soul feels like leaving and re-entering the body.

Fear of abandonment for me stemmed from many sources and layers in this lifetime and others, so it was harder to heal. This was a process of healing one level at a time of insecurities, fears, embarrassments, and blocks to love and trust. This fear would have been easy to stay in for the rest of my existence if I had allowed it to be. Luckily my Divine purpose outweighed my resistance in this area, and I kept going further—even when the amount of love I was now feeling in my life made the fear of abandonment much worse. The more you feel, the more you can fear losing if you stay in this. That is why there are so many people stuck in this paradigm. I asked God for a lot of help on this one. Eventually I had to surrender to this and let it all go. This was probably one of the biggest game changers of all the fears. You start to have real faith after this one, knowing that you are in the arms of the Lord and can fall into those arms and expect to be supported. It may take some people a whole lifetime to heal this one, but do not judge how long it takes you as it is your journey. Following are additional ways you might work on lowering your instinct or fear level.

Removing Fear Steps

Step 1: Ground and Center – Picture yourself connected by a column of light from the top of your head directly up to God/Source/Universal Energy. Allow that column to continue through you down to your feet and into the Earth connection of Divine Source Energy.

Step 2: Take 3 Breaths in Your Power – Below your belly button is your place of power. To get yourself into your power, be in the power of being ready to defend and protect your loved ones or remember a time when you were brave or had to protect someone. Breathe in three times. You will feel it.

Step 3: Lower Your Instinct – Holding a Limonite crystal will help lower your instinct, meaning your fear or fight or flight response. Picture that the fear is being lowered to the proper level for you so you can continue.

Step 4: Free Your Energy – Your energy is locked into the fear, and you need to get out of that mindset, so you say, "Free my Energy." This will allow you to disconnect from it momentarily.

Step 5: Release Your Fear – Allow the fear to rise up to God so that you no longer hold it.

Step 6: Believe It Worked — Have faith the process worked in every cell of your body.

Step 7: Fill with Unconditional Love — Allow yourself to be filled with the unconditional love of the Creator of the Universe.

Step 8: Test the Fear — You can try to put yourself back in the place of fear if you would like to test to see if it worked. When it works, you can't get back into it. In some cases, the fear is necessary for your life path or to keep you from doing something you shouldn't.

Using a Crystal Combination to Calm Fear

Dolomite Marble – Left side, waist level
Black Tourmaline – Right side, waist level

This may help when releasing fears from clients or while working on your own ability to work in new situations that cause fear. Its calming effect allows you to work in lower vibrations, and it disconnects the power of fear from the Heart Chakra.

Avoiding Fear in Areas Where You Don't Need to Go

I have worked with many students and apprentices who have wanted to get clearer answers and more information when connecting with their higher Divine Guidance. I have also worked with students and clients who were not comfortable with how much they were feeling or with experiencing other people's energy. Both had unique reasons for either feeling less or more than they would like to. The answer for everyone is to limit the amount of energy you are reaching out to hear or know when it is not aligned to your purpose or truth.

When I first opened up to Spirit, I was sensitive enough that I could feel not only Spirit but other things like the EMFs around anything with electrical or other energy running through it. Walking over water mains would cause pain in my lower back. I could sense the energy of light switches, which would cause a heavy feeling at my Heart Chakra. I was able to feel buried electrical lines, emotions, past lives, rivers, and any electromagnetic-powered devices. I sensed different beings, elemental spirits, false spirits, energy vortexes, energy signatures of earlier events, as well as energy from cemeteries, books, and religious items. I remember being overwhelmed and not knowing what to do when too many spirits came looking for help. Additionally, danger and warning signs were enhanced. Many times when Spirit was near, my heart would start racing, which left me feeling very ungrounded and unsure of my gifts. Eventually, I learned that it was not necessary for me to interact with everything I was feeling.

If I could go back and tell myself something that would have made all that time of learning easier to deal with, I would recommend asking my Higher Guidance to align my perceptions with my path so that I would only experience what I needed to experience. I would encourage asking God/Source to allow me only to interact with what was in my highest good and not a waste of my time. I would also advise asking that all of my Higher Guidance be aligned with my path and what God/Source allowed to be with me.

You can start by having the intent that you will feel, know, or experience only the energy you need to feel or experience. State that this applies to you and your family, home, cars, vacation places, shopping trips, workplace, and anywhere else you or your family frequent. Have these places cleared and adjusted for your energy before you even get there. Have anything that you do not need to know about be sent to Source first and not to you.

Ask that no spirits, including deceased family members, be with you unless it is aligned with your path and Divine mission. Not every family member on the other side will have the same vibrational level as you and will sometimes be working on themselves until they are ready to move to the higher realms. This is not your responsibility, and in that case you will not have to feel that lower chaotic energy. This does not mean that you can't talk to your loved ones, but just have them there when they are supposed to be there.

Developing Ways to Interpret Information

In my experience, I became aware of so many cases and energy related to missing persons that I did not know what I was supposed to handle and what not to handle right away. There was so much coming in that I could not focus. I had spoken to numerous spirits without knowing that they could lie to us, or that they might not be the spirits I am assigned to help. Much of my initial learning was coming from the advice of others, who were not able to help with my unique gift. When I was able to get answers from my own Higher Guidance, I did finally learn that most of the energies were not necessary to feel. Everything changed the day I could hear a simple "yes" or "no" from my Higher Connection. People will get yes/no in various ways: using different pendulum swings, hearing a telepathic "yes" or "no," seeing a visual "yes" or "no" with eyes either open or closed, etc. There are also levels of yes/no that can be discerned by some individuals. You can pull oracle or angel cards to get answers as long as you are not picking from your Subconscious Ego. If I pull a card when I am in Inner Child energy of the Subconscious, I may get a more fear-based card instead of the higher Divine guidance of Source.

Information comes in so many different ways. The visual clairvoyant part of my gift initially was only during deep meditation or dream state. Now it is with my eyes open or closed. Feeling was always my strongest method of getting and understanding energy. It is still the way I can sense the smallest vibration being off when working with clients or students.

Visual Signals

I had been open for a couple years before I started seeing sparkles of different colors in different situations. I did get my eyes checked when this first started happening because seeing with your eyes is different than seeing in meditation or with your third eye. My eyes were fine and there were no physical issues to cause me to see sparkles. I grounded myself in this case by asking my Guides what each color meant after I would see it. This is my code:

White – Angels
Gold – Guardian Angels
Red – Spirits that need to go to the light
Black – Dense energy or sickness, lower-vibration beings
Blue – Elemental spirits, such as Fairies, Tree Spirits, Nature Spirits, etc.
Green – Guides
Light Purple – Archangels
Deep Purple – Ascended Masters and Saints
Orange – Extraterrestrials, Alien energies

Occasionally these colors blended. I began seeing black sparkles around the heads and energy fields of clients coming into my office. I first saw Angels around people in this way.

Initially these energies would be visible for a short time, but eventually I saw the colors in more definite shapes and for longer periods of time. I have seen full figures for short glimpses, and this gift of "seeing" with open eyes keeps evolving. I do not seem to have to work on it, but it evolves with the work I am doing.

Auditory Signals

An ear tone is the only signal I hear audibly. This began for me as either a deafening sound in one ear or as ear tones. I had been told that's what happens when a nerve dies, but this was different because it occurred when I was working in an environment where the vibration lowered quickly. I asked my Guides about the ear tone and the meaning:

Ear tones — Indicate the vibration of a space has lowered quickly or to pay attention.

Body Signals

I learned my body signals and their meanings by experiencing them, not by having my Guides dictate them to me. One of the earliest signals I programmed occurred the first time I tried to locate a missing person who had connected to me in spirit. I had a "knowing" of where to drive to start looking. I had a chest crushing feeling while going over a bridge with a river below, so I went to the area under the bridge. I noticed this sensation in other nearby places. This feeling would be something that I continued to have experiences with until I could see a pattern to be able to understand what it meant. At the time I had only been open to Spirit for a few months and did not have clear communication with my Guides. I allowed myself to learn by experiencing because it was all I knew at that point. I was trying to figure out how this new skill operated. I allowed Spirit to show me important connections and lead me on interesting journeys, while along the way I was learning how to communicate with my Higher Guidance.

One morning I woke up hearing the audible words "Herkimer Diamond." One of the few times you will hear an audible voice is when just waking up. I decided to look up this crystal and to get one that day. I read that its energy could help with my psychic skills, and that was reason enough to find one. Luckily, my husband has been supportive in this growth and willing to go with me on these excursions. We found a store that had Herkimer Diamond earrings, and we bought them.

The salesperson recommended a lake for us to see while we were in the area, and we went on from there. Here I learned about the difference between an actual spirit that you could speak to and an energy signature that is left on a property. Additionally, there were Elemental, Fairy, Elf, and Tree Spirits, who also have their own energy signatures. I could feel the differences in the vibrations. I did not necessarily believe in Fairies and Aliens before I opened up, but made sure I opened my mind to hear these answers, even if they were beyond my beliefs.

Many of my days of learning how to communicate with my Higher Guidance were spent doing what I considered to be fun adventures to see where Spirit would take me. Who would we meet? What new tools would we discover? It is easier to learn when it feels like a new game that you learn how to play as you go forward. It was fun to see what the Guides would teach me next. I even learned how to decorate my office and center artwork on the wall without measuring. I have also been lucky enough to have a husband who is still in law enforcement because this allows me to learn signals for applications used in street patrol, drug investigations, and criminal investigations.

I am listing the body signals that I have programmed over my past eight years of coaching students, doing readings, and working cold cases and missing persons investigations. In addition to these signals I am able to get answers and more information by asking my Higher Guidance. You are welcome to use the same codes I use or a version better suited for you, your path, and your needs. I would also recommend dowsing charts to help if you are working towards opening up or gaining insight without a major shift in your energy. Each new level you reach will seem like starting over. Each time you master a new skill, Source will move you to a higher version of what you already learned. Being grounded may bring you back to the basics of grounding and centering at each new level you reach.

Codes for Body Signals

Energy is NOT YOU – both feet vibrating (one of the most important feelings)

Yes – energy moving upward to the top of head and above (strength determines level of Yes)

No – energy moving downward towards tailbone and below (strength determines level of No)

Deception or Holding Back essential information – sluggish energy at throat

Suicide or Feel Responsible for their passing – squeezing at throat

Theft or Stealing – both hands vibrating

Human Remains in the past 20 years, not accounted for – hands and feet vibrating

On Target for Human Remains (exact location either in person, on map, through other people, or by other means) – hands and feet vibrating with squeezing tight feeling in solar plexus (levels changing as you get closer) or your own specific feelings for this situation

Individual with Fear or Rapid Heart rate – racing heartbeat

Illegal Drugs present or being used – left foot buzzing to just above the ankle (stronger for larger amount of drugs or a drug dealer)

Amphetamines possible – racing heartbeat combined with Illegal drugs signal

Heroin use or on person -- left foot buzzing up to ankle with needle-type pokes in the left toes

Crack Cocaine or Methamphetamine – top teeth, all sensitive

Residue of Crack Cocaine or Methamphetamine – lower teeth sensitivity

Weapon (knife, gun) – top tooth left of middle teeth sensitivity (left lateral Incisor)

Stroke – left arm and leg numbness

Money involved – right palm itching

Tattoos or Piercings – light pokes and energy specific to location on the body

Drowning – coughing with a wheezing feeling

Hearing Impaired – silencing in the ears

Blind – blurred eyes

' Cancer – tight feeling on left side of the abdomen combined with other areas to indicate location

Illnesses or Injuries – pains in affected areas of the body

Heart Attack – right arm numbness and chest pain (feet buzzing = "It's not you.")

Married – left ring finger pressure

Mental Illness – left eye and left temple area, light pressure

Pregnancy with heartbeat – tightened abdomen with feeling of an inner heartbeat

Area of Concern – energy running up and down like an alarm

Police officer – clockwise feeling at throat with an up and down feeling at the head, like a siren (good to know if you are speeding and approaching a radar/laser area)

Tornado Warning – up down alarm feeling from the throat to about the top of the head (early warning system)

Pain in different organs – have to be programmed and retained if you do not know about the human anatomy

Use your own needs and ideas to add or delete from the following list of signals to aid you in energy healing and spiritual work. It is fun to work with your Higher Guidance when programming these signals as they do have a sense of humor, too. You can have as many signals as you can remember.

Energy Healing and Spiritual Specific Signals

Anger and Hatred – left of Heart Chakra

Guilt – right of Heart Chakra

Jealousy – left side at waist level

Envy – two inches right of Jealousy location

Greed – right side at waist level

Generational curse/Thought form – pokes on top of right hand

Place where the Soul is Seated – larger area left of Heart Chakra

In your Soul Body – tingles in both arms and legs (It is impossible to be in Ego when in your Soul body. You may feel this when doing healing work, meditation, other spiritual work and activities.)

Clearing Spiritual or Emotional Blocks – gurgling in the abdominal area (different than normal stomach growls), coughing, yawning, and taking deep breaths

Past Life – pressure behind left ear

Spiritual Attachment/Spirit Entity in field – left hip connection pain

Spiritual Attachment of Live Person – right hip connection pain (example: obsessed lover)

Open Portal (when it is not supposed to be) – uneasy feeling in Root Chakra

Closing Portal (when it should be closed) – uneasy or closed feeling in Root Chakra

Connecting with Your Path

Prior to my awakening, I had had very limited spiritual training and no guidance in the use of mediumistic or psychic skills, so as you can imagine, it was quite an ordeal. Opening up to abilities and knowledge that had not been in my awareness has caused some concern in various areas of my life. Without a spiritual focus, I think grounding would have been difficult. My focus was mediumship and missing persons. That is how the Universe decided to open me to the higher realms of who I actually am. My purpose as a Soul and my focus in this Earth experience led me to this path.

The case that I opened up to in 2007 was the disappearance of a mother of two, married to a police officer with whom I had worked before I was old enough to get hired as an officer. I remember having "ride alongs" and booking suspects with him. This would seem to be enough of a connection for me to recognize that the Universe was submersing me in this case, but there was more. This officer also worked with and supervised my husband through the time that the man's previous wife was found deceased in her home and now when his current wife was reported missing. As I watched the search unfold along with everyone else, I not only felt the presence of my friend Barbra, who had died two days before this woman's disappearance, but also the spirit of that missing young mother. This is what happened to change my life direction in a way I would never have predicted.

I decided to offer help in missing persons cases even when I was not fully aware of my gifts at the time. I just knew that if I was supposed to do this, it would happen. My taking these chances, when I might not have fully felt ready, expanded my consciousness each time. When I would feel pulled in a direction, even though I was terrified to make a mistake or to be wrong, I took action anyway—not because I wanted to, but because it was what I was being guided to do. For a while, I could only hear my Guides clearly in dreams. With time and experience, I learned to hear and sense in other ways. Being able to travel outside of your comfort area will allow the kind of growth that I have been privileged to experience, if it is aligned with who you are as a Soul and is not just coming from your own wants and Ego. I have seen both sides of this.

I started to see the larger picture of why not everyone can effectively do this work. I also noticed that some miraculous occurrences would happen when no one was paying attention or it was not a high-profile incident. Finding things and missing, endangered, or wanted individuals often happened accurately when only one or two other people would ever know. I discovered that it was possible to look at a map and tell exactly where the missing person was at that time and where they would ultimately be found—exact and in the way I would expect someone with my ability should be able to provide. Right?

I have given many locations that jurisdictions either could not search or that did not make sense to their case, so they could not search. I have also given locations that were completely off (by my definition). I have learned methods to be able to work with investigators when they can't discuss their case or evidence. I have spent time with some very devoted investigators who were willing to work with me when there were no other active leads.

I realized that you need to have God/Source's permission and blessing to work these cases and that you need to be certain that they are in alignment with your Soul's Purpose and work. Many times I have been asked to do missing persons cases or mediumship readings but have received Higher Guidance that they were not for me to do. I have learned that all things that are in alignment and that I have direct permission from Source to do turn out for the best and highest good and are not a waste of my time and others' time.

I may have been a little bit misled by wanting to help in areas that I was not always able to help, but I learned valuable lessons as a co-creator in this Universe. This has taught me that sometimes the higher road is to let go of something not meant to be and to grow in all other areas of my life in order to achieve clarity and peace.

There were times, sometimes daily, that I wanted to quit pursuing the original plan of working on missing persons and cold cases. Every so often I would ask God/Source to allow me to leave this path, but I was led back to it. I had achieved clarity in so many other aspects of spirituality, personal growth, healing, other realms, and more. Why didn't this area I had awakened to and was meant to work in grow at that same pace? I often wondered and cried about this, while I felt extreme loss and pain for the families, policemen, and investigators who were trying so very hard, just as I was. I spent years learning by searching for the missing person I had originally opened to. With high hopes for finding her, I searched any areas close to the visions I had received and wherever my Higher Guidance took me. I have never expected to feel good about finding missing people, but I feel compelled to follow my chosen path with God/Source, an extension of who I am as a Soul.

As a Soul you feel these things so deeply. When I was certain I had cleared any attachment to outcomes regarding these cases, I still was not to quit. I have looked in the eyes of people who are hurting so intensely from not knowing where their loved one is. Sometimes I can do nothing but be there for them like anyone could. I see them continuing to search whenever they can find time with hopes that they might find them. I watch the posts on Facebook of those wanting to know what happened to their moms, sons, daughters, spouses, etc. It is heart wrenching to not be able to do anything at that moment to bring them peace or knowing. I have worked with all levels of police departments, public and private investigators, and the FBI. I have driven to locations in and out of state to try to give any investigative information that would help them open their thinking to another possibility of suspect, motive, or other pertinent information.

On one occasion I had the OK to read in person at a police agency for a missing child case. As usual, I showed up ready but not really knowing what Spirit would allow me to see or do. One investigator, my husband, and I were in the interview room. Because I had previously met with the investigator and let him know that one of the ways I could receive information was to hold items to read from, he had a transparent evidence bag containing a large stuffed animal waiting for me. Seeing the toy was a harsh reminder that we were there because a young child was gone, and his family had endured years of wondering what had happened to him. In order to be able to read, I had to separate from this childhood belonging and from the fact that one of my own children was of a similar age and appearance to this missing child. I also had to isolate my nerves because not everyone is open to what I do to read energy and connect with the Divine this way.

I held the evidence, began to sense different energy, and then connected to what occurred with this child. I relayed the information to the detective. Because of the ongoing investigation, he was not able to fill me in on details, so I had to give information in a blind, anonymous manner. He could not react either way to whether I connected to the facts. I just needed to have faith and do what I was supposed to do without attachment, fear, doubt, or need for validation. I was able to walk into a nearby room and point to a place on a map connected to the child. I pointed to the same place on two different maps turned different directions. I connected, told the investigator, and left. As soon as I made it into the parking lot, I started crying and cried for hours after this because it was sad. No attachments or fear, I was just sad that this child endured something that should never happen to a child.

As far as I know, that place was not searched because it did not make sense with the other evidence, and to this day the child is still missing. I have to be able to walk away when it is time. I haven't forgotten, but I disconnected from the energy when I was finished.

Teaching with Spirit

Being aligned with Spirit brings perfect Divine timing into your practice. We grow in the areas where we need to grow when we listen to Spirit. Several years ago I began advertising classes that I was intuitively prompted to teach. I've moved to larger office spaces as the attendance at these events grew. I am looking forward to this opportunity to share with you the methods and techniques for teaching from Spirit that I have learned.

Opening to Your Path Exercise

Step 1: Imagine you are an open vessel for the Universe.
Step 2: Expand your consciousness to a level that you can co-create with the Universe.
Step 3: Be free of all of your Earthly needs when making this connection.
Step 4: Move outside of you and what you think the answer is.
Step 5: Explain why you are here.
Step 6: Listen to what the Source/God/Universe tells you.

Seeking Clear Guidance

Clear Guidance starts at the Heart, travels to the Solar Plexus, takes in a small amount of creativity at the Sacral, goes directly to the Crown and then out into the world. You owe your students the clarity of a teacher who is without ego, jealousy, obstacles to growth, or pre-conceived ideas about the students. Hold no stereotypes, money-based fears, judgments, biases, or self-centered reasons for being there. Place everyone on an even playing field. Even if you don't personally care for the energy of a person, you have to be willing to acknowledge their connection to you and why they make you feel the way you do.

Do you feel the reflection of their unresolved anger issues or childhood traumas? Do you feel past, present, or future lives affecting you? Do they want to become something other than themselves? None of this is your business when teaching from Spirit, unless it is done in a positive, uplifting way. Unless you need to take action in a group and are apprehensive about doing so, you should not feel any stress or energy beforehand.

Many times you are going to be lifted to a higher place of consciousness after teaching these classes, so you may become aware of your own related blocks. Your Subconscious will often try to keep you in a familiar Subconscious Loop of distraction so that you stay where you are and do not develop further. Your Higher Self may be afraid of growing at the Soul level and will also attempt to stop this growth as they may not believe you are ready. If you feel people who are jealous of you or have anger or hatred towards you, you may feel energy trying to stop you. This energy is not actually stopping you, but you may feel paralyzed by your own reaction to allowing in the knowledge of when people hate or dislike you.

You will have to adjust your energy the higher you go with your Spiritual connection and Divine mission. What this means is when the smaller holes of imbalances reach higher levels, you will become very aware of them and need to heal, close, adjust, transmute those parts of you to keep a centered, healthy mindset and connection.

Aligning with Spirit

1. Secrets – Do not keep secrets buried within you. I have watched many people torture themselves by holding secrets within their mind and Soul. Please acknowledge these to your Creator and release them for good. If Karma is connected with these secrets, you can still feel much clearer and freer by releasing them to the Universe. You are never required to say them out loud—just to God/Source/Universal energy. If you feel the need to apologize to Universe or to agree to make the situation right, do so.

2. Spiritual Boundaries – Keep healthy boundaries between yourself and your students and clients. Having a close inner circle is important to ground and focus on your mission. When we start bringing students and clients into our inner circle, we will feel the distraction. This does not mean not to care about people, but how will you keep the boundaries between work and free time if there is no line or definition between them? You will still help friends with their lives while keeping focus on your reason for being here. We can become lost in other people's chaos if we are not careful. Meditate to see if you need to fine tune this area.

3. Money and Payment – Allow yourself to achieve what you are allowed to achieve in this area. If you are focused strictly on this area, you will never achieve. Success will happen naturally as you become more and more aligned with Source. If we are focused in competition and lack, we lose that Divine higher connection. This is an easy place to navigate when you let go of attachment to outcomes. Are you willing to do a class for free if Source asks you to? Are you willing to request payment from someone you feel sorry for if Source asks you to? I am not saying this is always easy, but will you overcome your resistance to hear Source? Meditate on this to see if it needs to be adjusted.

4. Path to Change – Are you willing to send a student to a higher place than where you are? Are you holding back to keep the student dependent on you, or will you push them further, knowing that they might become better than you? This one has been the easiest for me. I feel this is what I do at the Soul level. This is the most valuable Spiritual tool you can give and receive. You become aligned with God/Spirit/Creator, free of attachment to outcome to be able to create amazing experiences for others. You find your way to release, surrender, and be at peace with the plan that is higher than you. Allow yourself to bring change to this planet in ways that only God/Source can bring through you and your Soul's purpose and Divine mission. Meditate on this and ask how you can be a clearer channel for this Divine transmission. This is the place of miracles.

Feeling the Power of the Room

1. Call in the God/Creator/Universe, etc. in the way that you do it, e.g. prayer, intention, crystal grids, bringing in white light, God light, Angels of the highest Divine order.
2. Adjust the necessary energies for the clearest connection for the group. It is important, however, to let the students be responsible for the energy they bring, such as Free

Will choices or any intended interference for your class. Let them sit in that energy as it is not for you to manage. Do the adjusting with intent. At times it might help to change where they are sitting. Have them wait outside if necessary. This is your Spiritual environment and Source energy will help you with this adjustment process.

3. Do not try to limit, block, or edit the Source energy as it comes through. At times we may try to edit the energy as it seems too "harsh" or moves energy and ideas with much more power and grace than we are accustomed to. This energy can feel similar to the fight or flight energy of adrenalin, but it is not the same energy. Much of the anxiety you will feel is your Soul Growth, not nervous fears. It does feel similar, but it is much different. If the only time you have felt this energy was when you were in conflict or trauma, it will be hard to let this through. Please use a licensed therapist to work on your unresolved fears and old hurts to become stronger in all areas of your life.

4. You will start to feel where the energy of the room is going at this point. Note there will be an easy and a more difficult choice to select. The one that creates the most change may make you feel a little nervous. Either choice will be beneficial; you will get another chance to choose the more difficult energy again at another time. The goal for the future would be to learn to trust the Universe to safely navigate you through the more difficult energy so that you will be able to choose that one first.

5. Connect with the students and allow the questions and interaction to occur. Release the need to know where the information is headed as it is your Higher Guidance navigating you through at this point. Following Spirit's lead is essential since you can't know exactly where this is heading. You will begin to trust Spirit after seeing the results of teaching from Spirit.

I have seen such amazing connections between students that I could have never realized on my own. Spirit finds the common link between the students and the Higher healing, clearing, and learning that is possible when we step aside and allow God/Great Spirit to lead.

Using the Power of the Voice

I have been using my voice as a technique to create change for most of my life. I am certain that all the trials of my life and police experiences have helped prepare me to transition into the Spiritual area. In most circumstances you can use a normal tone of voice and reason with people. I can ask, and they answer without resistance or fear. As we are navigating spiritually, there are times when we must get closer to an area of resistance for the person. As you get closer to this place, your energy will adjust to allow you to move forward safely.

An individual will on rare occasions say something to get you out of alignment and take you out of your power so that you will stop pursuing the line of questioning that is uncomfortable for them. An example of someone attempting to do this happened during one of the monthly healing-by-donation days that I host. A woman, who had been to my office before, wanted a meeting with me even though other practitioners were available to work with her. I told her that I would only be seeing those people Spirit decided I needed to see that day. These are the ones that I can benefit the most and who are in Divine timing to make the change that they need to make.

She stayed the entire day, waiting for a turn to have a session with me. During the afternoon, I walked by her to check the sign-in sheet. She stopped me and said, "Put your shoulders back." I asked her what she needed, and she showed me with her body how I should stand up straight, while repeating, "Put your shoulders back." At that, I slouched forward a bit more and said "No." I added that I was happy with how I am and that I had been working over people all day. I explained that with the mild scoliosis in my back, my posture was what felt most comfortable for me at that time. I could feel that she was attempting to take me out of my power by trying to find an insecurity or imperfection in me.

At the end of the day, the last practitioner was working on her, and Spirit asked me to go sit by her to continue the conversation. I asked, "Why did you feel the need to tell me to put my shoulders back?" She said she was trying to help me. I asked her why she needed to say something to correct me that even my friends would not say to me. I let her know I was aware that she was doing this because she felt the need to take me out of my power since I was not going to see her that day no matter what she did. I was staying aligned with Spirit. She jumped off the healing table to face me, "How dare you accuse me of trying to take your power." Screaming and throwing her arms around like a small child, she continued, "How dare you." She left, and I heard her continue to shout in the hallway until she finally exited the building. All this time Spirit was telling me to hang in there.

A few minutes later she returned from the parking lot and pointed at me, appearing to be crying but with no tears or yelling. I asked her, "Do you want to hug me or hit me?" She said "I don't know." I told her, "You came back, which will allow me to remove old energetic patterns from you at this time." She said she would just make an appointment with the other practitioner at another time. Because I was in my power, not Ego, and clearly hearing my Divine Guidance, I had to tell her that there was not a practitioner, other than me, who could clear this particular past life energetic pattern from her. She left, and I have not had contact with her since.

Being Brave in the Face of Conflict

I continue to trust Spirit even when a conflict occurs because I see the need to uncover energy that at times is hidden by Free Will choices. If God wants me to let his power speak through me, I adjust my thinking and do it, even when it is uncomfortable or feels stronger than I am.

Spirit has occasionally made me aware of new individuals in a group who have self-serving motives for attending. When I lead groups, I accept the responsibility to take action when prompted. There are times when people make substantial spiritual breakthroughs, which make them vulnerable for a few moments while opening to this new energy. I have always been aware and protective of this when working with students.

On one occasion I questioned a woman about her spiritual practices, and she claimed to sit in public places and take other peoples' energy as sport. Individuals like her try to tap into others' spirits in order to power themselves without having to grow spiritually. This does not work for very long for the person tapping into others' energy.

When you see, sense, or know that someone is draining energy from another in a group that you are holding, first check with Spirit to know if you are to intervene or not. Sometimes this is not for you to act on. It will be clear to you when you do need to act to protect another. Energy draining is noticed at the Root Chakra most often or in the grounding cord to the Earth and purpose. If Spirit needs for you to have someone leave a class, it is usually without incident and fees can be returned to the student when they leave.

I felt uncomfortable the first few times I had to ask people to leave. When I was able to see that the reason went far beyond the student and me, I understood a bit more about what Spirit was doing. Instead of being uncomfortable at witnessing this, others in the group said watching me in my power, handling the situation with composure and dignity, made them realize they were capable of handling struggles in their lives. It gave them permission to be in God's light and power in order to correct energy that was out of alignment with them. They said they were feeling empowered.

I have discussed this with classes when these things happen so that they can experience through me what it is like to stand in their power. Being alone in the front of the room can be a scary experience when you need to do something uncomfortable in your power. Trusting in Spirit will lead to positive experiences when you do what you are aligned to do as a Soul. Being true to who you are as a Soul allows you to make changes in energetic patterns and allows you to teach others this way of being as well.

Following is a process that you can do now to prepare for the next time you need to be in your power. Because you will have already had a practice run with this, you will know that you are not experiencing fear but faith.

Being in Your Power Exercise

Step 1: Open your Crown Chakra to God/Source.

Step 2: Breathe in the energy of this Divine connection so that you may be aligned with the true Source of All That Is and Will Ever Be, the I Am energy of All That Is.

Step 3: Imagine all parts of you being aligned with your purpose and mission, and feel the peace that being this aligned creates for you.

Step 4: Feel the God/Source energy preparing you to power through an obstacle with Divine grace.

Step 5: Note the power of this force and sit in this for 3 minutes until you feel attuned or used to this energy.

Step 6: While in this energy, perform an everyday task like reading the mail or calling a friend.

Step 7: Allow yourself to be raised to the next connection of Divine spirit and love, making this process easier in the future.

Step 8: Thank Source for this opportunity.

Being brave is a powerful advantage to help you in your spiritual path. Source will give you direct guidance regarding when and when not to take action.

Creating New Connections within Your Scope of Reality

Once you have realized that being uncomfortable leads to new spiritual connections, you will not mind these situations so much. At first you may feel uncomfortable, annoyed, attacked, fearful, lost, or out of sorts. This is what new growth feels like. I have often asked Source, "Do I need to feel this uncomfortable energy?" and Source advises, "Yes." I will sometimes get an indication through a programmed pendulum swing or body signal of a past life, so then I will ask, "Is it mine?" When I am told that it is not mine, I ask, "Do I need to sit in this?" and get a "Yes." After dealing with this over time, it seems to get old.

During these times, I just kept telling myself that it must be necessary to endure this for my growth or higher connection. There came a point where I finally had fulfilled what was necessary in building the new connection and was able to have that portal closed. I am grateful that I do not have to access that doorway any longer.

Even when the human mind does not understand, we have to have faith that there is no other way to bridge the two worlds of information without some growing pains or discomfort. We weren't built to be able to access these areas with a human mind, but only with our Soul body. The human body is extremely limiting for what we do and know as a Soul. Humans and other living species are based on survival programming. To create a new connection in order to be able to access higher levels of ourselves and our divinity, we have to learn how to bypass the drama and other negativity that attachment to ideas and things has created within the human experience. Although the human experience is at times loving and safe, we are constantly reminded of how very short life is and how vulnerable we are. In these fears we will never bypass the human brain.

Experiencing Temporary Physical Symptoms Related to Attaining Higher Connections

Make sure you first check with a medical doctor before you believe that any physical symptoms you experience are due to Spiritual awakening. Then, do as I do, and check with your Higher Guidance to determine if it is necessary for you to feel this. If not, ask not to feel it. At times there may be no other way but to go through the process, or it may serve another purpose, so if the answer is yes, ask when it will be completed.

Headaches – I often experience head pressure or a mild headache when accessing higher realms that I have not reached before. You may even feel mild pinprick-like sensations on your head as the Crown Chakra opens or updates your energy for new connections. If you are sensitive to headaches, you may have more during this transition. Check your chakras and make sure they are all open and spinning clockwise. If not, breathe in light to all the chakras and ask that they be energized, cleared, and balanced.

Sudden Onset Crying – Sudden openings of the heart and solar plexus can create crying spells in some sensitives. There were times I would be crying for what I thought was no reason. My Higher Guidance let me know that I did not have to know why and that I would feel better afterwards. The strongest crying spells I have is when God/Source cries or when I can feel the Angels cry. Check your chakras when this happens to make sure they are all open and spinning clockwise.

Anxiety from Soul Growth – Sudden onset anxiety when there is no reason to be anxious or afraid is often a sign of upcoming Soul Growth. As you approach a new level of growth, the closer you get to it the more anxious you become. It almost feels like you are in danger, so if you know you are not, you just need to cross the threshold of the Soul Growth. To do that, picture a finish line, a hurdle, or a similar image. Intend to cross it. See yourself running, walking, crawling or being carried by God/Spirit into the new area of growth. At that point, all you have to do is allow the new energy in, and the anxious feeling will fade. You may step up now to do something new, teach a new class, or accomplish a precise goal. The Soul Growth feeling is not a signal to stop short. Please keep going when you feel the support of the Universe behind you.

Reading Energy Using "Escape Your Mind and Learn to Fly" Phrases

The forty-seven "Escape Your Mind and Learn to Fly" words or phrases were designed to allow you to fully open areas of your intuition and mind that are blocked or not accessible to you at this time. This is the system that I used when working with my Higher Guidance to overcome blocks and to move my physical mind aside and grow spiritually at a much faster pace. Just picking up this book will automatically connect you to Source/God/Universal energy and will ground you to the Earth and your current lifetime. Each word or phrase has an activation on a higher level, which you will feel if you are sensitive. You may notice subtle changes in your intuition right away.

The first time that you read this section, sit quietly for a few minutes in peace or meditation while still holding the book. Trust that your intuition will allow you to receive what you need at that moment. Listen to your Higher Guidance to allow more information in. Later you can look through the descriptions and experiment with different ways of reading yourself and others.

One way that I have used the "Learn to Fly" phrases is to have them professionally printed for my students to use as oracle cards. You can easily make your own deck by writing each word or phrase on a 3 x 5 card. Choose cards from the deck, letting your intuition guide you in selecting the appropriate number of cards to give you information for your current energetic body or question. Trust that you will receive what you need at that moment. Listen to your Higher Guidance to allow more information in. Check the descriptions in this book if you feel drawn to do so. Allow yourself to invent your own way to use this information and to have fun while learning.

Action – is the next substantial step needed to move forward. Action does not always have to be physical and can be changing the way your view something.

Balance – is an ideal state of taking something from imbalance to balance; equalizing; balancing chakras.

Being Thankful – accept what you have as enough; give thanks.

Being Trained – is anything that is new that you have not handled before, an educational experience, or practice.

Change – is transformation, the moving of energy into another form.

Clear Subconscious – clear or remove hidden meaning in the mind that is not serving us any longer.

Connecting Energy – is any energy that you connect with such as family, friends, co-workers, bosses, strangers, or an energetic area of responsibility by contract with God/Source or others.

Crown Chakra – represents our God/Source connection.

Feel Love – being able to open your heart to a higher level of love is the key to spiritual connection.

Fly – accept and honor who you are as a Soul and fly to new heights.

Forgive – let go of anger, hatred, or other hurtful emotions you are holding and release to God/Source anything you cannot forgive.

Free Speech – say what you need to say.

Free the Way You Think – release your current mind set.

Free Will – it is your choice. You won't miss out on something if you choose not to do it.

God's Pocket – indicates you are as safe as if you were in the pocket of the Creator. Believe you are protected.

Heart Chakra – relates to the ability to love and receive love being directed at you.

Hummingbird – savor the sweetness in life and be able to change directions quickly and without effort when necessary.

Inner Child – is influence from unresolved childhood fears.

Jump – power above your known reality to the true reality of space/time.

Just Wait – take time.

Ladybug – a wish was heard and answered.

Light up the Truth – when the truth is masked or not easily read, Source can light up the truth for a clearer understanding.

Limited Information – is an area where you currently do not have access to information.

Listen – allow yourself to sit quietly and receive a message.

Lower the Thought Form – remove a strong belief system that is no longer serving you.

Lower Your Instinct – allow your fear threshold to be lowered to a level that is in balance with who you are as a Soul and why you are here in this lifetime.

Mirror – isolate your own energy from other influences by picturing a mirrored ball around you reflecting that energy away from you.

Mirror the Way You Feel about Receiving Important Information – in order to be able to access a clear answer, isolate your own energy from the influence of your Ego and Inner Child by picturing a mirrored ball around you reflecting the influences of other energy away from you.

Not You – is a way to know that the energy you are interacting with or feeling is not yours and belongs to another person, place, or thing.

Past Life – is a lifetime other than your current one.

Path – relates to your life path, i.e., what you came here to accomplish or experience.

Penguin – represents endurance.

Powerful – own your own power.

Read the Way You Feel – take a moment to sit and see how you feel.

Release – let go of something that is no longer serving you.

Ring a Bell –open another doorway for yourself by ringing an actual bell or by just having that intention.

Root Chakra – relates to your connection to the Earth.

Sacral Chakra – relates to your connection to creativity and sexual energy.

Separate Energy – ask or intend that multiple energies be separated so that you can identify or work with them.

Smell the Roses – notice and enjoy what you already have; taking time for yourself.

Solar Plexus – relates to self-importance and will.

Third Eye Chakra – relates to being able to receive clear psychic or spiritual information.

Throat Chakra – relates to verbal or non-verbal communication.

Trust in the Will of God – trust that if God wants it to happen it will.

Turn Switch Off – turn off non-beneficial sources' access to your energy or another's.

Vows/Contracts – are anything communicated with the intention of following through with an action or energetic tie to another.

Woodpecker – is a sometimes uncomfortable amount of changes or healing coming that will pass in time.

Powering Through Resistance

I am looking from one place and trying to force my way through to the next. This type of thinking is not working, yet I persist. I ask God for help to get there faster and stronger. I pray for this accomplishment, not knowing God's plan for me. When you decide it is time to do something, it is not always in your best interest to achieve it at that time.

Often you will exhaust years attempting to bring about things in this manner. This is what Resistance and a Subconscious Loop can create. Do you want to reach your goal, or do you want to prove that your way is the right way? Proving you are right is in the Ego portion of the mind. Your Resistance originates in the Ego. Stop trying to force growth from the Subconscious Loop since this will never work. Even though your human mind thinks it is a good idea, the Creator/Source understands you and what your Soul plan is.

Growth is often the plan. Growth requires you to step back and assess what you have accomplished and to plan for the future, taking into account the balance and Soul experience you need. Every Soul wants direction. If it does not feel this direction, it often loses its clear connection to where it comes from. When this happens, fear, displeasure, and suicidal thoughts and actions occur. You tell Source, "I want to be left alone," and you disconnect from your Source. Even though the human part of you may feel free to disconnect, your Soul will be out of alignment with path, and this will be felt at the human experience level as an unidentifiable, underlying, painful emotion. Numbing this pain becomes your goal, and you may lose lifetimes before regaining your footing as a Soul.

Souls are made of many parts or aspects, all aligning to the Creator level. Branches of your Soul may be in other realms or dimensions, all working to grow and support your fellow man and the energy of the Universe. Being a Soul that is not aligned is like having a cold or sickness in part of the Universal energy. This Universal energy, sometimes called Higher Consciousness, All That Is and Will Ever Be, God, or Source, is collective and includes all of your Soul parts, your fellow man, light beings, aliens, planetary alignment, dust, termites, molecules, atoms, and beyond. You cannot segregate at that level. You will not be able to disassociate from the energies and people you do not like there. Your thrown stone ripples beyond this world and into realms the human mind will never be able to fathom.

The mere idea that we are physical has nothing to do with being physical in the larger Universal scope. You will never understand the true paradigm of life. Creatures that live and breathe are living in your realm, but they are not living when you look at the larger picture. Source is the living, breathing Spirit, and we are living here trying to learn to support and become this energy. Much reprogramming is necessary, and the realms that you create in your mind's eye increase the distance between you and God.

Disassociating from negativity is negativity. We indeed need to change how we see resistance. Resistance is a dream we have without knowing what we are, where we came from, or where we are going, when we indeed have no clue. Perhaps plugging ourselves in with faith, love of fellow man, loss of fear, and loss of attachment will allow us to ride the light of the Divine, the Divine particles, so that we can create a balanced paradigm here on Earth and in other realms. The key to overcoming resistance is to quit trying to figure it all out. Align with the Highest. Don't pretend to know everything. Leave some room to grow. Enjoy the ride.

Using the Subconscious Codes Wheel for Healing
(View a Larger Chart on Page 87)

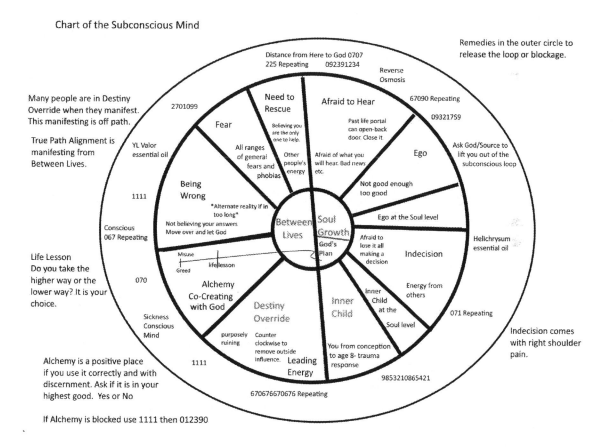

Chart of the Subconscious Mind

The Subconscious Codes chart can be used by holding a pendulum over the center and allowing it to swing to the areas that need reprogramming, healing, or correction. You can also use the chart with your own eye tracking by allowing your eyes to relax and intuitively move to focus on the relevant block and then the correction. Your pendulum or eye tracking might indicate several areas if you are in the full Subconscious Loop that tries to distract and disrupt you right before big changes.

For proper manifesting, the goal is to be in Between Lives or Soul Growth, which make up the center circle of the Subconscious Codes Wheel. You are where you are supposed to be if you are getting a clockwise pendulum swing in the center circle of the chart or if your eyes are focused in the center. You may also be on the line crossing Between Lives and Alchemy. A Life Lesson or challenge in this lifetime is indicated by a vertical line on the Alchemy co-creation line.

The next ring or layer of the chart deals with areas of the Subconscious: Fear, Need to Rescue, Afraid to Hear, Ego, Indecision, Inner Child, Destiny Override, Being Wrong, and Alchemy. Alchemy is the only Subconscious manifesting on this level that is positive. When the Alchemy energy is being used properly, it will be indicated by a pendulum swing from Between Lives out to Alchemy. A counterclockwise swing in Alchemy means misuse of this energy, such as energetically harming others or yourself out of anger, revenge, fear, or ego.

To find out whether thoughts that you are unsure of might be coming from your Subconscious, hold the pendulum over the chart's center and see where it swings. If a Subconscious block is indicated, allow the pendulum to swing over the outer remedies to correct it and allow you to be free of this mind block. The outer circle contains all of the remedies that have been revealed to me so far for correcting some of these areas. The most effective remedy, however, is to ask God/Source to pull you out of the Subconscious distraction you are currently in.

Using Subconscious Codes to Escape Your Mind's Barriers

If you are tuned in to your own Higher Self, you may already be hearing your Subconscious. Development of spiritual practice should always include linear (a bridge from one realm to another) escape plans from the messages of the Subconscious mind, which function to keep you in what is considered to be a safe place based on lifetimes of survival experiences as a human being. Humans have always been challenged in their existence, so this DNA-type programming has developed over time. Experiences with the Divine, however, require you to bypass the normal operating system of the human brain. Think of times when you have been ready to do something new in this lifetime and have had the feeling of being frozen.

This is the human mind. Most times you can use the strength of your will to push through to accomplish whatever it is, while continuing to experience a small amount of fear.

Soul Growth is the area that you will experience if you are aligned with what your Soul and God's plan are designed to do so that you stretch your Soul to a new level. This growth can be felt on both the human and the Soul levels. Fear will always be present right before this type of growth, along with a chain of distractions we will call the Subconscious Loop. For the purposes of keeping the Subconscious journey as easy as possible, we will refer to 11 main areas.

1) Soul Growth

This is the largest bump of spiritual growth you will encounter while on Earth. It is the reason you exist here. Each bit of spiritual, emotional, physical, and mental growth that stretches the Soul to God/Source is considered Soul Growth. Just growing here at the physical level in this lifetime is difficult, so imagine how your Soul feels when pushed further than its current level. The Soul also encounters the unknown and experiences fear just as we do here, but at a more extreme level than compared to a single human lifetime. When you reach these areas of growth, your Higher Self and Source may have different views on what is the best course of action.

I will always side with Source. I need to have that higher direction by God/Source, which even has my Higher Self learning and growing at a fast pace. We will see how much is possible in each lifetime if we stay aligned with the Higher Truth. This may feel like you are fighting with yourself at times, but don't assume your Higher Self knows more than you do. You have the ability to move up to the level of your Higher Self much faster right now because your Divine mission has you energetically charged to lift the planet's vibration, which means you can get in some much needed Soul Growth in this lifetime and upcoming ones.

When you feel stuck and in that feeling of fighting yourself, allow God/Source to raise you to the place where you are aligned and directed by God/Source instead of just your Higher Self. Soul Growth feels like danger and fear when there is no reason in your physical world to feel that way. When you feel Soul Growth, just breathe through it and ground yourself with the truth of your safety. If you feel guided, use this prayer of affirmation:

I am here fully supported by God and the Universe in my path. I am the director of my own truth and destiny. I co-create positive change for myself and others through manifesting my full and undivided spiritual truth and

**existence. In all directions of time, I am free of unauthorized attachments and
fears misdirected by lower entities or lower places of existence trying to move
me to an unfulfilled destiny. I am free, clear, and directed by truth from this
day and into all time/space continuums.**

2) Between Lives

Between Lives is a place where plans are made and details are secured for another
Earthly life, assignment, or direction of your energy. Choices are made and independence is
gained by agreeing with God/Source/Universal energy on upcoming events and assignments
before you enter a new realm. It is really just a void in between assignments—like a hallway
to the next place you are going.

Committee often meets here to help you understand why your growth depends upon
certain circumstances and changes. Committee is your Soul team working under the direction
of Source's highest energy. In visions or dreams, you may have seen such a meeting or round
table discussion with your Guides and Mentors. While still keeping you grounded to your
Earthly needs, your committee decides your highest path to change, growth, and desires
as a method of changing old patterns from previous places of your Soul's existence. This
is also known as the Life Lesson. Re-establishing your core Soul beliefs and focus in your
current lifetime is usually the Life Lesson, the area where you focus on creating positive
change while still maintaining your goal for the lifetime being discovered.

If you are in this place on the chart, this means something is being amended or altered
to work with the changes that the lifetime has already brought about. You are recalibrating
to the current energy and not what you originally came in with. In other words, you may
have earned the easier way as you have mastered your Life Lesson.

When in your Life Lesson on the pendulum chart, there is a higher way or lower way.
When you have mastered the higher way, you earn the right to change your destiny. In other
words you are co-creating a better outcome, or an outcome that was not planned, with God/
Source/Universal energy.

God/Source/Universe's Plan

God's Plan on the chart means you are in the beginning stages of co-creating with
Source. This is where you are asking for a purpose, goal, and direction that you would like

to experience because you have already mastered the Life Lesson pertaining to that area for this lifetime. For example, if financial burden or lack was scheduled to help you grow in an area of greed or mistrust, you may have found your truth and the highest part of your Soul, and you may even have helped the Soul level to grow. If this is the case, you may have earned the right to manifest or co-create with God an abundance of finances or dreams that were previously outside the original plan for this lifetime.

You will then move into the Alchemy section of the chart and will not stop on Life Lesson. The pendulum will swing energetically on that line between God's plan and Alchemy. If you overstep, you will end up in misuse or greed with a counterclockwise swing. If this happens, pray or meditate on this issue in order to find your own individual remedy and life purpose work to be done. It is OK to want more, just be aligned with your destiny and direct Source guidance when wanting more.

The counterclockwise swing on misuse or greed might have another cause. Others may be trying to use your manifesting to benefit them. This will slow down your manifesting if they are using your energy for this purpose. You will not be held accountable, but it will slow down your co-creating power with Source.

3) Alchemy

This is a powerful, positive place of the Subconscious mind that anyone can access. For this place to accelerate your path, you have to be knowingly creating. As with all good things, there are instances over time where people have misused this area. It must be used with respect because of the Karmic consequences, which are extreme and painful. Do not divert from your intended path when using this place.

Alchemy is defined by my Higher Guidance as "the ability to resurrect." Resurrection comes in various forms and conditions. It is intending for the Universe to reverse its original plan in order to bring a new and improved plan forward. Decades ago there were secret societies that practiced this craft with hopes of healing, inventing, creating, and stopping the spread of evil. This power is extreme and requires patience and time to develop.

I have used Alchemy to prevent harm from coming to others in this lifetime without knowing that was what I was doing. My intended purpose was to prevent further harm, and in most cases this worked. Those who hurt others are already open to Karmic penalty, but Alchemy is not a part of Karma. This Subconscious place is a loophole to ancient secrets, past life knowledge, and the ability to concentrate the power of the Divine with the rational human mind. Many mistake this knowledge as words of God and will misuse it to attempt to overcome races and religious beliefs. Aligning one's path with what God has created with you will keep you from misinformation about the generations of Alchemist proprietaries. Much of New Age technologies are made from Alchemist ideas, Rife, Biofeedback, water generators, flower essences, homeopathy, and so much more.

Life Lesson While in Alchemy

It is possible that your co-creating may be delayed while working on your Life Lesson. Some people have many Life Lessons to master prior to being able to freely manifest. Manifesting or co-creating with God/Source is very powerful and the areas of greed, jealousy, misuse, and Life Lessons must be mastered in order to do this the proper way.

If you are angry, envious, jealous, greedy, hold hatred, or are not connected to God/Source when using this chart and Subconscious clearing method, you may be misusing or co-creating with non-beneficial entities or energy depending on your life path. All of these areas must be mastered to properly manifest from the highest possible light. The choice is always to take the higher way or the lower way, and you just have to choose. Do I choose the right way or the wrong way? Will it be God's way or my way? Mastering your own wants and needs and applying that knowledge to make a higher decision and connection is how you will master the Life Lesson. That is the truth of manifesting. Doing the opposite is Destiny Override.

4) Destiny Override

When you end up in Destiny Override in your Subconscious mind, you are purposely making decisions that are separating you from your intended path—sabotaging it with your own Free Will. It is easy to end up here because sitting in the energy of the intended change is often hard for one to manage. It feels like being lost or in painful discomfort from change and growth. You get to one point where you are manifesting, and then you become scared of this new energy at the Soul level and will often divert or not trust the plan. That's when you push through your own ideas of what will work. This allows you to manifest the wrong outcome. Other people's ideas and strong beliefs may also pull you in this direction. If an outside influence puts you here, you will have a counterclockwise swing in your Destiny Override part of the chart. Ask God/Source to pull you out of this so that you can continue with the intended manifesting in the area of Alchemy.

When you feel lost, understand that this is the normal process you need to master to get the intended new information. Feel lost. It is OK and necessary. When this feeling comes in, just sit in it for five minutes and allow yourself to move upward and forward. Feeling lost is powerful, so that is why you wish to get out of it. Sit now for five minutes to move forward from all of the lost experiences in this lifetime. You may see times when you were a baby and no one came to pick you up when you should have been, or when you were a child lost in a store, or when you grew older and didn't know what to do next. Do not study the information, just allow it to run through and carry you to the next place or level of vibration. Not all uncomfortable energy and feelings are bad. In fact, a higher, newer level of love in your heart will always be painful. Feel it. It is why we are here.

5) Inner Child

In most lifetimes, the Inner Child will need work and guidance as you move to develop further. The Inner Child can be defined as the consciousness you created in your early years, usually between being in utero and the age of eight. It has often been thought of as the inner youth. Conscious creating starts at eight years of age unless sudden trauma or unseen circumstances occur that create a need to accelerate growth in order to obtain safety within. The Inner Child years are when you are most dependent on the outer physical world to support you. Based on different variables, you may need to retrace the route back to Inner Child to create a void (empty out the trauma memory) where the unforeseen circumstance occurred and reconnect the accelerated adult manifesting model.

Things the Inner Child may communicate will vary depending on circumstances within the Soul. Irrational fear-based thoughts and ideas are common. When paired with Ego, we call this paranoia. The Distance from Here to God 0707 code will release the bond between Ego and Inner Child at the Soul level.

If you have discordance in your current human lifetime, you will have another level of Ego and Inner Child as a bonded pair at the Soul level. If you pair Inner Child with Indecision, some hoarding and schizophrenic behaviors may become apparent. The 225 repeating and the Distance from Here to God 0707 codes will likely lift you to be able to hear the reason for why this is currently in your consciousness so that you can heal, release, and escape from the thought forms.

Some areas of the Subconscious can create very large and powerful thought forms. These are often the basis for long-term mental illness or depression. All areas of the Subconscious can be mastered and moved through and away from with practice and healing on all levels.

Inner Child at the Soul Level

By imagining all of the lifetimes and places in time that you have had a human mind and an Inner Child part of the Subconscious, you can understand what makes up the Inner Child at the Soul level. It is the accumulation of traumatic and extreme changes that the Soul has experienced as a child. When explaining this to students, I say it seems like a large, angry baby, but that is not always the case. It is not an entity but more like a file cabinet drawer of information that pops open unexpectedly when a trigger causes it to open. This means that you have a pattern of misalignment in your life asking for help subconsciously, which opens the power of this set of experiences stored in your Soul. This is never a positive place even though you may feel a mild relief from whatever experience you are in when this happens. If you find yourself in this area, picture the drawer of records that opened by itself and then just close it. You will be able to change the pattern when you identify the trigger that opens it.

The power of manifesting poltergeists and other emotional energy forms is in this section of the Subconscious. If you feel that you may have manifested out of fear, just ask the Universe to return anything you sent out. You can picture a vacuum at your solar plexus bringing back anything that you sent out accidently.

6) Indecision

Indecision is the Subconscious belief that you are going to "throw it all away," to be without. This area includes distractions your mind has for dealing with yours or others self-respect issues. "Crying over spilled milk" fear will hold you hostage, and you will be afraid to advance in all areas of your life. In order to access information or experiences never before experienced by the Soul, you must master this Subconscious area. The way one would bring through another's energy in this space is by your inability to make your own choices and always looking to see how your choice will be approved or needed by others. Your choices are yours based on your needs and your God/Source connection. These decisions need to be for your highest good without wasting your own time just to benefit others. People often feel pressured by others when deciding because they need it or like it, so they choose that way instead of their own way according their alignment with Source.

All of the advancements in science and the medical field come from people who can move freely out of this area. New concepts and ideas reside here. Learn to master this level in order to be free of other people's energy coming through and throwing you off course.

Energy can easily come through during your dream space or when you are actively dreaming. You may experience others' dreams instead of the ones intended for you and your Soul purpose. This information may make you feel that you need to act when it is actually the other person you are pulling through. You may wake up thinking the problems of another person are yours. You may feel your life path being altered when it is just another person's space you are allowing through your own indecision.

When you see this person, it usually will remind you of an aspect of yourself where you still need to focus attention on growth. You feel a connection with the person as they are as much or more indecisive than you are. You decide to help them with their issues before working on your own. You then become bonded in the fourth dimension of change and growth, creating a path of toxic energy that is allowed to pull between the two of you.

This usually happens in pairs and not a large group. Although this can affect a large group if a teacher is misusing energy and guiding you to false hopes of change and growth through ego-based healing techniques. Group empowerment or success themed classes are susceptible to this. The remedy codes for this are: 067 repeating, Distance from Here to God 0707, 071 repeating, Reverse Osmosis, 225 repeating, and 067 repeating.

7) Ego

Ego is the powerless place you go when you think you are more or less knowledgeable than you think you should be. Second guessing is common in this place as well as overachieving syndrome. The Ego is often afraid it will be found out. In other words that people will know who we actually are.

Experience in dealing with Ego will come when you realize this voice is not God, or a Spirit Guide, or a deceased relative that crossed over to the other side. It really is just an insecure part of us that brings uneven energy and chaos into our lives. Most people will not be comfortable when a person is speaking from their place of Ego. Very talented scam artists can use the power of Ego to trick you into believing what they are selling is real. You will feel uncomfortable with them being in Ego, but a part of what they are saying will be attractive to you. Trusting your gut comes from dealing with a person speaking to you in Ego. You will feel internally that something is off even though there is something irresistible on the outside. The uneasy feeling is there for a reason. Take note of it and pay attention. What you see on the outside of people who are stuck in the Ego part of the Subconscious is often not a true reflection of who they really are. Part of this is also the Ego at the Soul Level.

Ego at the Soul Level

Ego at the Soul level consists of all the Ego parts of the Soul from all lifetimes and places of existence in all directions of time and space. This is really just stored information that shows up when a complicated part of the Soul space allows this information to emerge. When stuck in the Ego, feeling weak or indifferent about a current thought pattern can bring this "drawer of information" into a person's current reality, causing them to seem obstinate, narcissistic, enraged, or stuck in their own ways more than usual. This energy will feel the way a bully would push energy around when they are not getting their way. Dormant anger may bring this part of the Subconscious forward, causing strife and chaos in the outer world through manifestations of their own inner fears and rages. Strong energetic thought forms can be created here without easy ways to dissipate them. For instance, a child may be in fear when they are small and feel that an adult is not protecting them. A child's strange visions and dreams can put them in a place to affect their outer world with their mind. This may be powered with the energy stored here in the Ego at the Soul level. If the Soul is not connected to love and light in this lifetime, they may bring the evil or negative energy of another lifetime into the present as part of themselves. Most Souls, however, do not have this part. If you become aware that this drawer has opened for you, just close it in your mind. It is not useful or constructive because manifesting here will not bring positive changes.

8) Afraid to Hear

When we dismiss the way Higher Guidance is directing us, we are in the Afraid to Hear part of the Subconscious. Information coming in is not what we want to hear, so we will block it out. Some patterns I have noticed in this area are people blaming others, being defensive, becoming victims of scams, and having manic episodes.

One example of Afraid to Hear that allowed me to see the importance of receiving a whole message occurred when a client needed to decide what to do with her marriage. We connected to God/Source, and she was to receive her message from Source. Every time she got close to the answer, she would be in Afraid to Hear. We got her through again, and she heard "Leave." She was very upset because she did not want to leave her husband, so she became very fearful of that outcome. I asked her to tune back in because there was more information. Eventually we worked through her block, and she heard, "Leave it up to God." That last part was very necessary for the client to have the full, intended message from God. What a difference a few little words made in this case.

A useless portal opens when stuck in Afraid to Hear. Past lives that do not need healing or attention will just randomly come through, leaving you more confused than when you first tried to access information you were afraid to hear. This is the only place that past lives can get through to our consciousness.

Another complication of this useless past lives portal is that entities or revenge seekers can use the opening to access this dimension's backdoor to throw you off path or make your life more complicated. I have seen people's deceased loved ones use this door when they have not gone to the Light or made the necessary reconnection to the true Heaven source after leaving the Earthly body. Because they do not check in with Source, communicating with people here is nearly impossible. If they can't attach to an energy field, they may not be able to use electrical connections to communicate. This forces them to either cross to the Light eventually or try to come in through a backdoor method. This section of the Subconscious is the only area that can be breached by those on the other side when they have not crossed over. This creates an attachment to the energy field due to the lack of integrity in a person's energetic field when this door is open.

Individuals on this side who astral project can also find this open door and use it to connect as an astral entity. Close the door permanently when you have mastered this area. The integrity of your field is assured when you are connected to God/Source and this area is aligned by that true connection of love in the most unconditional way possible.

9) Need to Rescue

The Need to Rescue part of the Subconscious is based in primal instinct. Need to Rescue is similar to fight or flight syndrome, but it is felt for someone else. This is usually based in fear and the belief that you do not trust in the Universe, or you do not believe that God/Source will act. I have watched group activities where the minute a person gets close to making a breakthrough, the Need to Rescuers will distract and pull some of the uncomfortable energy from the person working on the breakthrough. That person will not have enough power to change if others are rescuing. If someone is not open to the enabling behavior, others will not be able to tap in that way. The reason they tap in like this is to prevent the person from being uncomfortable. What they actually are doing is preventing the energy of change needed to break through.

If you tend to rescue, look within for anything that is not healed. Let others fully feel the energy of change. You are not helping when you try to take the edge off for them. Helping people is allowed, but this area of the Subconscious is just an energy field, so there is really nothing tangible to rescue them from. Just allow the change for the other person. Breathe through the feeling if you sense it strongly. You will also grow if you can allow them their change while breathing through your own discomfort, without acting on it.

Some people will have throat or lymph node issues if they are in this area for an extended amount of time and energy. This includes breathing issues such as asthma or some types of cancers including lymphoma. Remedies include the code 225 repeating or sealing the place on the bony ridge behind the left or right ear with Frankincense oil. Iolite and Black Onyx will help to balance the Need to Rescue area enough for you to navigate out. Sometimes adding Snowflake Obsidian will increase the power of these crystals.

10) Fear

This area includes all ranges of fears and phobias.

11) Being Wrong

Being Wrong is a part of the Subconscious fear area specifically related to making mistakes with decisions. Did I make the right choice? Was there another way? This is second guessing in the area of the Subconscious that will place a limiting thought pattern on each obstacle. You may even cause changes and some mild manifesting of Being Wrong when locked within this area. If you try to create a new connection, this area can stop you for many years as it is one of the most powerful areas of the Subconscious to escape from. If you want to move beyond into faith, this is a key area to focus on correcting.

If faith can heal, we need to believe that all we are creating and healing is coming from Divine Source. Anything less than true belief and faith will lead you to this area of Being Wrong. This is the part where you move over and let God. The trickiness of this area is that it creates new dimensions within and out. One can manifest a new area of disability in Being Wrong. That basically means you create another dimension of the Subconscious in the category of Being Wrong above and below, which makes it even more difficult to bypass that programming.

Remedies to assist you include the Distance from Here to God code 0707 as well as the combination of the crystals Black Onyx and Snowflake Obsidian. These will only work if you have mastered the work within required to bypass this area.

If an imbalance in life is combined with Being Wrong and Ego, certain aspects of narcissism become apparent. Ego and Being Wrong lead to a fear-based approach to all decision making. New ventures are nearly impossible, and the fullness of a steady, loving, balanced life is difficult to achieve. To fully clear being stuck in this thought form combination, healing work will need to be done to repair a marriage, grieve a lost loved one, or deal with unresolved trauma.

Leaving It Up to God

The inner circles of the Divine depend on God/Source to guide their mission. Sometimes what appears to be a roadblock is actually a diversion to a more acceptable approach. There may be obstacles that cause concern, but nothing will prevent you from achieving your destiny. Even fear can only hold you for so long before you enter the area of your Spiritual Destiny. Fear is not Divine Love and won't keep you from succeeding.

When God Puts You in a Time Out

I have had clients who've been put in a time out either by God or by their own Soul. Not every Soul will be placed in that area where God won't answer you, but almost everyone is open to that possibility. You remain connected, but you do not hear the response to your questions or prayers, when before you had. This usually happens for things like not listening or for any of the spiritual blocks caused by anger, greed, hatred, or neglect. I can feel when a client is not being communicated with from the God/Source level. I personally find this devastating to feel because I know how important that connection and voice are to your Spirit and destiny while here on Earth. Without it, I would not feel aligned and centered in my Divine faith.

One way to tell if you are in this space where God/Source is not responding to you directly is if you feel it at the Soul. The Soul is seated to your left of your Heart Chakra. When you ask, you may feel that area constricted or not flowing with energy. Often a person can apologize and make a promise to keep from entering those spiritual self-blocking behaviors. It is not up to me, but I ask God/Source if it can be changed each time I am aware this is the case for someone I'm working with.

When Your Soul Puts You in a Time Out

I recently learned while working with a client, that her Soul had discontinued direct talks and connection when she continued her Free Will choices that were hindering her path. Through negotiation with both sides, we were able to come to an agreement where the Soul returned.

I asked if this had ever happened to me, and I was told that I have not had a God timeout, but that when I was ten years old my Soul had temporarily disconnected me from my normal awareness and connection at the Soul level. I couldn't think of what I had done wrong at that age and could not find anything to explain it. When I was able to clear my own thoughts and ideas related to this, I finally heard the truth. My truth.

When I was ten, I remember the day my mom, who was an alcoholic, was extremely sad and crying in her room all day. She ordered me to take my five-year-old half-brother to the park to fly kites. I recall feeling that something was extremely wrong because she was crying at a level I had never seen before. I told her I wanted to stay with her, but she must have refused because all I remember after that was taking my brother to the park. We played and came back home to my mother being placed into an ambulance and us staying at the next-door neighbors' house. I was always told she was taken to the hospital because of her drinking, but as an adult I learned by chance that she had shot herself in the chest with a handgun that day and had almost died because the bullet came within a close proximity to her heart.

As I have been rising to a higher level or vibration since opening up, I noticed I was sometimes crying for no reason. After I realized I was not connected to my Soul during that incident, I decided to ask if I needed to be reconnected to what had happened in that time and was told, "Yes." I sat in meditation with the intent to open what was missing from the time the Soul was not with my body. Much of what I felt was physical discomfort in the Heart Chakra, the realization that my mother had to have surgery, and an awareness of being in the surgery room. I was able to see energy clearer after this session. A surge of higher vibration was able to radiate through me and into group events in a stronger and more defined way than before.

Experiencing Your Spiritual Destiny

Experiencing your spiritual destiny requires focus on the positive aspects of your existence as well as the evolvement of your life from where you started out to what you have become. It does not mean that you have perfect surroundings, finances, health, and support or that you live without fear. It means that you are willing to get to the next level or vibration of your Soul destiny. Part of a Spiritual Destiny is the knowing that comes with making it to the next step. I know I have made mistakes. I know that the other methods of achieving what I want are not working, and I am willing to allow myself to reach up higher than I know in order to be able to achieve what I can't at this current vibration level. In doing this reaching, you will have to overcome not only yourself, but your Subconscious mind, previous knowledge, friends and their expectations of you, and your own version of your truth. This is a very difficult task and is seldom done without a great effort of endurance and love. You are going to have to connect with what you believe is higher and at the highest vibration of love. I call this God/Source, but you may say Goddess, Universe, Sun, Stars, etc.

When you are connected to this God/Source energy, you have to ask for what it is that you are looking for as far as development and change. After that you have to be willing to hear the answer to why you are currently at this vibration, what still needs to be mastered, and what God/Source has planned for you and your Spiritual growth. Sometimes this means you will hear that you will experience more of the same until you have learned what lessons and parts of your puzzle are required to move on to the next step.

Many times you might feel like you are ready to give up on the learning process because it is too difficult, and you just can't take it anymore. The truth is that these are the times when you are getting closer to the next level. You can choose the easy road and go the other direction, but in reality this is not the easy road. You will be doing the same as you have been doing for whatever extended period of time you have created, or you will identify this as approaching the top of the level you are at and realize that you need to push through the known to the unknown. Pushing through the barriers of your Ego mind and the beliefs that you have always had will allow the Soul Growth it takes to move forward to another level of understanding of why you are here and what you represent in the larger scale of existence. Are you brave enough to see what else is possible, or do you stay where you are?

Even if you decide not to push forward, you will always feel that push to see what there is beyond what you know, and you will be pulled back there numerous times in your current lifetime. You have to really want to push through. It is part of the process that was set up to protect us from knowing too much before it is time. When opened too quickly, people may become depressed or appear to be mentally ill without the proper grounding and timing to be able to grow.

Sometimes chronic hallucinogenic drug users have visions that they are not supposed to have because they were not opened to destiny properly due to damage to the part of the third eye/brain that allows this grounding and centering to happen before moving forward. I have seen a pattern of previous hallucinogenic drug use in clients complaining of seeing only evil and negativity with their gift. This is not considered a gift, but with the right energetic healing from the right healer, they can become more aligned with what they are supposed to see. Drug use may open the third eye, but know that it is not meant to be opened that way. The process is there to protect you. You must knowingly go forward and unlock these gifts when you have mastered the teaching needed to ground and center at the level you are currently at.

Understanding this will help you understand why some people seem to open up more quickly by adding accelerators to their growth. Some people will open up because of circumstances, but those circumstances are always planned by you and God/Source. You can't will it to happen. It has to be in the Spiritual Destiny assigned to you and only you. Stretching your spiritual muscles is possible for anyone who puts in the effort to grow. This does not mean you can accomplish what you neighbor is able to do with their spiritual gift, but it allows you to stretch what part you own and can manage through your own truth. In other words, do not compare gifts as everyone is different. Celebrate the uniqueness of your gift and the special way God/Source connects with you.

In this book you will see little pieces that connect with you while still celebrating the way your own information is sensed by you. If you can see that you already have everything within to know what your next level is, you will quit asking others to tell you what that is or to direct you to it. They just simply do not have permission to see your path. Only you do.

If you can release the ideas you have for what you think the answers are in order to hear the actual ones from God/Source, you will finally be able to assess if you wish to move to the next level now or not. This, after all, is your choice. I am merely here to make you aware that the difficulties are there on purpose so that you don't accidentally open up to more when the foundation is not there yet. It starts to make more sense if we see it as a protection, like a childproof lid on a bottle of medicine. When you are grounded and centered enough to know when or when not to open the lid, you will be given the knowledge to be able to move the lid the appropriate way to allow yourself to reach the next level.

LESSONS FOR TEACHERS AND STUDENTS

Breathing Activation Techniques

<u>Lesson 1 - Learning to Breathe in the Creator Energy</u>

Sit comfortably in a chair or on the floor.
Listen to the sound of your surroundings—all the sounds and distractions.
Let those sounds recede into the background and know these are familiar, safe sounds and good to keep around you.

Make a full connection with your tongue touching the roof of your mouth.

Sit and listen to your breath.

Let your breath and abdomen move as they do naturally.

Feel the deepness of your Soul connecting to your Third Eye Chakra.

When you feel your belly full of energy, lower your jaw so that your tongue is not connected with the roof of your mouth. This allows the light of God/Source to fill you fully and deeply within your Soul.

Do this for three cycles with the tongue first connected to the roof of your mouth and then lowered. Advanced students, use your own intuition for the cycle variables.

Lesson 2 - Expansion of the Consciousness

Take 5, deep, abdominal breaths in through the nose (expand abdomen, count of 10-12) and out through the mouth (count of 6-7).

With your mouth closed, connect your tongue to the roof of your mouth.

Breathe normally through your nose until you feel relaxed and slightly elevated in vibration. Slowly breathe in and then hold your breath for a count of 35. If you can't do this right away, don't force it. Those of you who are centered and able to sense the energy will feel it connect at 35 and raise you up, expanding your consciousness, removing limits of your human mind and fears.

Sit in this energy and breathe it in. Allow any information to come to you from your Higher Self or Source. Just being in this place will help you energetically heal on all levels of your being. You will eventually be able to stay at this vibration in your everyday life. This takes time, so please do not be discouraged.

Lesson 3 - Manifesting with the Divine Plan

Sit relaxed in a chair.

Cross your ankles. (It does not matter which one is in front of the other.)

Be aware of your throat and your Throat Chakra. Picture the blue color of the Throat Chakra spinning clockwise as it should.

Be aware of your Solar Plexus Chakra (stomach). See the healthy glow of the yellow gold you have within, moving clockwise, creating changes for the positive in alignment with your path.

Take 5, deep, abdominal breaths in through the nose (expand abdomen, count of 10-12) and out through the mouth (count of 6-7).

With your mouth closed, connect your tongue to the roof of your mouth.

Breathe normally through your nose until you feel relaxed and slightly elevated in vibration.

Picture the connection of your Soul body (left of Heart Chakra) and your Spiritual Destiny (left hip area) and gold from the Solar Plexus, all connecting to the left side of your neck (Throat Chakra).

Any blocks in this area will feel like being off or a mild discomfort at that time. Open your eyes and focus on a point on the floor or wall and hold that gaze until the discomfort stops.

Close your eyes and breathe in 4, deep, abdominal breaths through the nose (expand abdomen) and out of the mouth.

You are now in the area to properly manifest the destined plan of alignment with God/Source for this lifetime. Just sit there and breathe, expanding the time spent here until you eventually bring it into your everyday world. This is not for you but for your destined mission and alignment with God/Source.

Lesson 4 - Becoming One with All That Is

First, complete Lessons 1, 2, and 3 (keeping ankles crossed) in that order.

In that elevated state of consciousness, see the entire world as white and gold; see it liquefy and then become mist; breathe in this white and gold mist.

Take 3 deep breaths.

Uncross your ankles.

With your mouth closed, keep the tongue connection at the roof of the mouth while taking 3 more deep breaths through the nose: in for a count of 6 and out for a count of 4.

Lower your bottom jaw until your tongue is not in contact with the roof of your mouth.

Breathe through your mouth for a count of 50.

Reconnect your tongue to the roof of your mouth and close your mouth.

You are then in your Soul body, feeling positive tingles on your extremities.

Keep breathing in and out of your nose (ankles not crossed) until you feel the lift of your Soul. There is almost a heartbeat feeling at this place of oneness. Stay there for as long as you wish. Eventually you will bring this into your everyday world. Watch what happens when you do this.

Lesson 5 - Experiencing Your Twin Flame Soul Connection

Do Lessons 1, 2, 3, and 4, and then start this one right after.

Sit in a chair (ankles not crossed) with your feet on the floor.

Make tongue and roof of mouth connection while breathing gently through your nose until you can connect with a feeling or knowing of a connection on your back, slightly to the right of your Heart Chakra. If it needs to be repaired, it might feel like a slight uncomfortable feeling. To repair, take 2 breaths in and out the nose.

Hold breath for a count of 25. (If you need to work up to this there is no hurry.) This will release any old hurt or connections of loss one did not see coming during this lifetime and others. Free of this injury to the Soul, you will become more aware of your closest teammate: the twin flame. Some will have more than one as they are all varying Divine plans.

Take time to sit in this connection. Healing on this level creates more energy for other projects; unhealed this area becomes a distraction for growth.

<u>Lesson 6 - Miracles of the Divine</u>

After you have completed Lessons 1, 2, 3, 4, and 5, stand facing a door with your hands above your head.

Allow your feet to be connected to the Divine by breathing through your nose for 4 deep breaths with your tongue connected to the roof of your mouth.

Lower your jaw so the connection is open and tongue is not touching roof of your mouth. Breathe out and hold breath for a count of 14.

Waves of energy from the Earth and your God/Source connection will push through any blocks and reestablish you in strength in every connection of your Soul and body: connecting energies, removing doubt, fear, and other vibration-lowering feelings or ideas. Faith will fill any voids or rough patches.

You will close your connection by touching your tongue to the roof of your mouth and placing your hands down at your side.

Breathe at a normal pace through your nose.

Allow God/Source to direct the Miracle through you and your Free Will.

Clearing Residual Debris from Astral Travel and Time Travel

We need to travel to other realms to create new spiritual connections. When we do this, there are sometimes small particles of residual energies that keep us from fully returning clearly. Interference from residual debris picked up during astral and time travel may stop you from doing your intended nighttime work with the Divine. There is an easy method to clear this debris with a strong magnet.

Hold a magnet over your right palm. To know which side of the magnet works, you will have to try both sides until you feel a pull in your abdomen (or use a pendulum to indicate). Once you feel this connection, move the magnet along your arm until you reach the top of your right shoulder. Direct the energy of the magnet in a clockwise circle (up to 30 times) above or directly on the right shoulder until you feel your Third Eye connect (pressure right above your eyes). This will reset your connection and remove any residuals from travel to other realms. You may have to do this nightly to be clear for nighttime travel.

Interpreting Dreams

In my meditations and connection with the Divine, dreams have been described as part of the conscious mind and not the subconscious mind. This means that dreams extend into our waking hours and are an active part of our consciousness. In order to evaluate what type of dream you are having, I will divide the information into six types. This is introductory information, and I will be going deeper into this area in the next book.

Dream Visions – are Divine visitations with loved ones, spiritual messages, and God connection information developed through one's ability to stay in a meditative state.

Déjà Vu – is anticipating events before, during, or after events either while sleeping or awake.

Past Lives – information from other directions of existence enters when the doorway to the Divine is open. This is also the place where astral travel is possible. Moving between spiritual realms and consciousness occurs here as a result of intention and great spiritual focus.

Regular Dreams – are made up of random recall of information. In the waking hours this can be confused with psychic information that does not make sense. In sleep it would be a release of built-up electrical impulses.

Conscious Mind Clutter – information is magnetic and collects similar experiences, so any traumatic event or quick change may bring this accumulated clutter to the surface during REM sleep.

Psychological Response to Trauma – is a dream state when you have suffered psychological stress, loss, or a mental illness state. This is where paranoia in the daytime will occur. Night terrors and other sleep disturbances are fear-based conscious reality that goes into the sleep state and conscious awake state.

How to Give Psychic Readings

Until you are used to being in the highest place to get clear guidance, you can use this pendulum chart to see if you are in the right place to do readings. Remember to always go higher than you think you can.

Vibrational Chart for Reading (diagram)

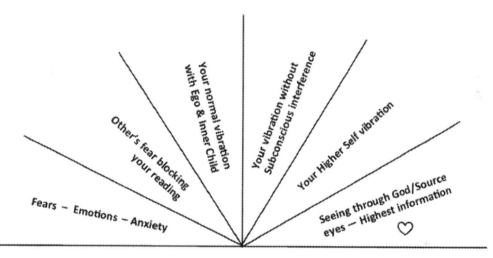

Your vibration affects the accuracy of the information you are getting when you read. Before you start, use a pendulum to get yourself into the area between Higher Self and God/Source. If your energy drops, pick yourself back up using this chart to energize your connection. Ideally, you will want to read from the Highest information area indicated on the right side of the chart.

Prayer-Love-Support

1. Connect to God/Source with your intent to help the client and not only yourself.
2. Connect to the information through oracle cards, prayer, the energy, etc.
3. Information should pull the client up higher; if it does not, don't say it.
4. Use common sense.
5. Refer client to necessary resources (therapist, doctor, domestic violence shelter, etc.)
6. Have a plan to deal with someone who is dangerous or suicidal. Safety is #1.
7. If you have trouble connecting, try holding the client's hand.

What to Say When Information Comes In

A reader should have the intention to connect spiritually at the highest level to help the client see the light for themselves in order to receive their own truth and guidance. This may require holding space, but sometimes it means you are energetically supporting their clear connection to the Divine that everyone is capable of having.

As Spiritual Intuitives, we don't judge. We don't bring our own unresolved issues, anger, greed, neglect, jealousy, guilt, religious expectations, or any other filter that will taint the clarity of the connection you are making for them. In other words you will need to be a clear channel of the Divine/God/Source/Creator energy. Focus on your connection to the Divine, asking to be brought up higher than your Subconscious and emotional filters to eliminate any spiritual or personal blocks you have to doing the reading.

When giving a reading to a client, there are many areas of information that you will need to rephrase in order to give an ethical and compassionate message. I am aware of psychics who have told people that they see cancer, tumors, the dog is very sick, etc. in ways that could get them sued. If you are not licensed to diagnose, cure, treat, or prescribe you need to be careful. Never tell someone who does not know it that they have cancer or a serious disease. Even if your gift gives you that type of information, delivering it improperly can be very harmful. Here are some options for how to say the same thing without the liability of diagnosing.

What not to say: You have cancer or other serious disease.

How to say it if needed: Advise where you feel energy is unbalanced and ask if it is theirs or someone else's connected to them. Because a person may be closely connected to someone else, you may not always accurately read that person. Do not scare clients because it will always stay with them. The idea or suggestion of serious illness is not beneficial to hear in that way. Encourage the client to always stay connected to their medical doctor and to have anything they are concerned about investigated or treated by a medical doctor. Encourage them to keep up with health screenings and usual tests and to listen to their body.

What not to say: Your husband or wife is cheating on you.

How to say it if needed: Unless you are a qualified therapist or social worker, you should not give marital advice. If your indication is that someone is being unfaithful, try saying, "If you sense that there is something to investigate based on your own gut feeling, check it out for yourself if you feel guided to."

<u>What not to say: Someone is going to die.</u>

How to say it if needed: If you get information that someone close is going to pass away, but there is nothing that can be done to change it, don't say it. The Universe will alert this person if they need to know. You can support them in connecting with the person if they feel guided to and they bring it up.

Free Will and Readings

Many times a client will not tell you what they do not want you to know. If they wish to keep their Free Will choices from you, God supports this unless someone else is being harmed and immediate action is required. You will most likely sense these choices if they are pertinent, but clear information will not come through. You may be aware of an aggravating circumstance but will not be allowed to access it without the client's permission. You can only read accurately for what you are given permission to read. You will have to ask the client to open up their energy field to include Free Will choices.

You can allow a client their privacy while clearing their energy block by having them think about what the possible incident or trauma might be. Having them concentrate on this allows the Universe to remind them of the information that needs to be released. Have them do this until your receive a signal that the client is in the right energy or tapped into the place where the information is stored. At that time, they will need to forgive, release, or any other way guided to correct the energy. This can all be done without you ever knowing what the client's personal information is. You can work blind like this very effectively.

Essential Oil Recipes for Room Sprays

When doing readings or any other spiritual work, you might want to use these essential oils for yourself or others. All of these combinations have been channeled from Divine Source. I did not see any reason to keep them to myself. You are free to make what you will with these. It is all good. I tend to use more Young Living Oils and FES Flower Essences since that is what I began with. You are really just looking for a vibration and scent that brings the energy you are looking for. I am not picky about oils, so choose what works for you. I usually use a base of distilled water and a small amount of organic vegetable glycerin as a preservative. Brandy, vodka, or witch hazel could also be used as the preservative. After making the sprays, I often add biofeedback frequencies and prayers, as well as allowing the healing energy of the Universe to charge the spray with the God/Source frequency.

Feel free to make the sprays in the manner that works for you. As with anything, make sure the essential oils do not conflict with any current medical advice or care. Have fun adjusting them with your Higher Guidance to make them what you need. I have always found it fun to see what Spirit can show me. Everyday amazement keeps me going and trying new things.

The drop amounts are for a 4-6 ounce spray container. I prefer dark glass bottles, but it is up to you what you use as your spray container.

Base for all sprays:

Distilled water
Organic vegetable glycerin (as preservative)

Note: A preservative is not needed when using flower essences, which contain alcohol.

No Limits Room Spray
12 drops Valor Essential Oil (Young Living)
10 drops White Angelica Essential Oil
 4 drops Palo Santo Essential Oil

All of the Above Room Spray
16 drops Inner Child Essential Oil (Young Living)
12 drops Angelica Essential Oil
 4 drops Thieves Essential Oil (Young Living)

Center in Love Room Spray
20 drops Rose Otto Blend (or 1-2 drops Young Living Rose Oil)
 3 drops Lavender Essential Oil
12 drops Sacred Frankincense Essential Oil (Young Living)
 6 drops Lemon Essential Oil

Faith Not Fear Room Spray
15 drops Myrtle Essential Oil
10 drops Three Wise Men Essential Oil (Young Living)
 8 drops Helichrysum Essential Oil

Past Life Clearing Spray

Use <u>Blue John Fluorite Elixir</u> as the base water. The indirect method for making the gem elixir: place distilled water in a glass container and allow it to float in the bowl of water containing the crystal Blue John Fluorite.

No preservative is needed in this blend because of the alcohol content of the flower essences.

12 drops Valor Essential Oil (Young Living)
12 drops White Angelica Essential Oil
 5 drops Myrtle
25 drops FES Five Flower Formula
10 drops FES Lewisha Flower Essence

How to Assist with Investigative Cases

When you find a missing person or cold case that you are interested in helping with and your Higher Guidance has given you the OK, here are some things that I have found helpful for working these cases. First, ask yourself the following questions:

<u>Should you be involved</u>?

1. Do you have permission from God/Source to assist with this case?
2. Do you put yourself or others at risk by searching or assisting in this case?
3. Do you have an unresolved issue that is similar or related to the case, which may cause you to misread energy?
4. Will you be breaking any laws (stalking, criminal trespass, other harassment, tampering with evidence, obstructing a police investigation)?
5. Are you attached to an outcome (finding the missing, being right, showing how well you can read, or having a preconceived idea of the outcome)?
6. Do you have any psychological challenges that make it impossible to read for other people?
7. Do you feel you are open to psychic attack or curses?
8. Are others using your gifts to get information for their own purpose (reward money, notoriety, etc.) by having you read for cases?

How will you do this work?

1. Will you work with Spirit Guides, Angels, or the deceased to gain information?
2. Will you use maps, eye tracking, pendulums or other means of dowsing, etc.?
3. Who will you give psychic hits to?
4. Are you able to discern helpful information from information that will just take up an investigator's time?

How do you feel after working with these types of cases?

1. Do you feel sick after these investigations?
2. Do you suffer attachments after this work?
3. Do you become violent, agitated, or depressed after the investigation is complete?
4. Do you feel any sense of paranoia after a session?

If you do not receive a "yes" from God/Source, any one or several of the negative outcomes listed above may arise. I have learned that if you don't have the blessing, you don't do it no matter what others pressure you to do, or you feel you must do. People who decide to do things without the backing of the Highest sometimes leave themselves open to failure or energy depletion. I have helped a number of individuals with these situations after they've participated in criminal or paranormal investigations when they shouldn't have.

Understanding Active Missing Persons Cases

When there is an active missing person search, the investigating agency will not have time for any intuitive or psychic information. If you happen to have a police officer or investigator as a friend or family member, they may ask you if they feel guided to. Many cases are solved right away or within a day or two when the person returns on their own.

I have had the experience of locating both people wanted by the law and active missing people at the time they were reported. Any pertinent information as far as areas the police should check may come to an intuitive in the form of psychic or mediumistic information. It is possible for information to come in so accurately that you can give a person's location and the time and place they will be found. I have even been able to see in-progress calls in my mind's eye—with the offenders running and jumping into a vehicle, which I can clearly see, and then speeding off. I have also been able to find locations by looking at a map and using a process I call Eye Tracking or psychic pointing with one's eyes.

The accuracy of the information a person receives is dependent on many things, but the most important is if God is allowing you to get direct information from Him. Accuracy is also dependent on how clear the person is as a channel. When you stay focused on helping the loved ones and solving cases, you become less dependent on what others wish for you to be or what concerns you have about how you might be perceived. Your path may not allow for this type of work, but you may decide to do it anyway. This does not mean you won't be accurate at all, but any information that would assist in solving a case or finding a person may be limited.

Programming Body Signals for Reading Investigative Cases

I have extensive programming for body signals that I use to receive and interpret information for investigative, mediumship, and other intuitive readings. If you spend fifteen minutes in meditation each day, you can start to program signals for yourself. Often you will discover that you were already experiencing either a psychic or body signal for some of these items, but you had not made the connection. Following are suggested information areas for you to begin programming body signals to use in reading investigative cases. These will give you one layer of information that you might also apply in other circumstances and situations, depending upon how you are using your gift.

Suspect
Drugs (heroin, cocaine, dealer amount, personal amount, or other you wish to program)
Weapon (can be specific to what type knife, gun, bat etc.)
Theft
Homicide
Suicide
Fled the Scene/Pursuit
In Progress
Vehicle (type and year or other information specific to what you investigate)
Tattoos (location on the body, visual of actual)
Gang (negative entities are always associated with gangs; isolate out before programming)
On Target (exact location, within the amount of miles, feet, inches you've programmed, of the person/object of your search)

Evidence (DNA, etc.)
Intoxicated
Blood
Specific Organs (kidneys, heart, lungs, spleen, skin, bones, etc.)
Specific Illnesses (heart attack, high blood pressure, cancer, diabetes, blood diseases, etc.)
Police Officer

Using Eye Tracking

Since my awakening, one way that I have naturally received information has been through Eye Tracking. I allow Higher Guidance to direct my relaxed eyes to something in my surroundings that either is the answer or that provides a clue to the incoming information. I use this when looking at maps, teaching from Spirit, gathering psychic information while driving (street signs, places, names etc.), choosing crystals, or other everyday tasks. I trust my Higher Guidance and do not block this method of information when it comes in. It is a safe and convenient method to use at any time because you maintain full awareness. You can even use it to find misplaced items such as keys, wallets, and jewelry.

To teach this to students or yourself, use a marker and a roll of paper to write the following word categories large enough to be seen at a distance. For investigative cases, you might write the following on several sheets of this oversized paper so that they can be seen at one time.

Directions (N, S, E and W and other directions you would like to include)
Months
Days of the Week
Holidays
Seasons
Emotions (Anger, Jealousy, Greed, Love, Sadness, Happy, etc.)
Elements (Fire, Water, Earth, Air)
Numbers
Years
Alphabet
Yes, No
List the Chakras
True/False

+ - < > = x

List of causes of injury or death

Colors

Descriptive words (Tall, Short, Flat, Oval, and other words)

List of Spiritual Beings (Angels, Loved Ones on the Other Side, Saints, etc.)

Boy, Girl, Man, Woman, Child

Relationships (Grandparent, Parents, Mother, etc.)

Spatial Relationships (Under, Over, Next to)

My "Escape Your Mind and Fly" Phrases (Free Will, Change, Listen, Path, Jump, Fly, Limited Information, Free Speech, Just Wait, etc.)

List of Mental Illnesses (Bi-polar, Depression, PTSD, etc.)

Meridian Underactive / Meridian Overactive

Outdated Vow or Contract

Bringing in Information

Updating Akashic Records

Non-beneficial Entity

Removing

Adding Positive

Open Chakras

Germs

Phobias

Fears

Realign Energy

Separate Energy

Cancel or Delete

Highest Good / Not In Highest Good

Use this system to get information, and eventually you will get the words in your mind instead of needing the word chart. This will improve your ability to use Eye Tracking information as you relax and allow the energy to come in. Just like with any other dowsing or oracle system, always see yourself as light, with the Divine connection within and with God/Source. This allows you to read accurately, without outside influences changing the energy so that you would not be able to read clearly.

Using Maps to Locate Items, People, or Evidence

You can use the Eye Tracking technique for map work. Another option is using a pendulum or feeling energy with your hand. Each one of these methods will take practice for you to perfect your own individual way of working. If you or the missing person has a past or future life in a location, you will have to isolate that out in order to get correct locations.

Be aware that energy is always moving. Your human mind will never be able to understand all the movement in the universe: planets, time, space, dimensions, and many other circumstances. This is where having God's blessing on these cases helps so much. Without God, it will be impossible to get exact information about missing persons or other cases. I guarantee it. I have a clear connection after years of clearing, fine tuning, etc. This takes work and dedication, and I still learn daily. Be OK with being given incorrect information, if that is what God needs to give you, so that you move or change energy, make a connection, learn, or remain safe. You may have an urge to give up or stop, but if you are meant to keep going, you will eventually hear that over your own thoughts of quitting.

Make sure you are clear and grounded. Limit distractions. Decide on a precise date and time that you want to receive information for. If you don't, you will get random information that includes incorrect information, which will only frustrate you and waste your time. Once you have decided on a specific time and date, you will have to have the intent of stopping time, and then picture coring out a small sample of that exact time to read from. Feel free to use multiple dates and times but only one at a time. If there is movement, you know the victim is moving or being moved. Many runaways will map out this way.

Ask that only God/Source guide you in the map work, and make sure you have the blessing to look in the first place. Program different pendulum swings if you are using a pendulum to show On Target, Evidence, Past Life, or any other useful swing you can create to make your understanding clearer. Know that sometimes a victim can be in multiple locations at once if they were dismembered or if evidence of blood/saliva is at multiple scenes. Try asking more specific questions. Don't assume you know immediately what you are receiving. This is a learning process, so stick to it until you understand. You can use this for treasure hunting also if you would like to try that.

Once you have the information, find out from Source what you need to do with it. Options would be to do nothing, give it to the police as a psychic tip, write it down and wait for the correct time, or write it down to keep as part of your learning process. You may also be directed to forward it to the family or a private investigator. My advice is to follow the Higher Guidance and to stay aligned.

Building Information Recall

Watching news clips or police dramas can provide good training in memory recall that will make you seem organized and professional in your psychic skills. Pause the show and try to remember what the person looked like and what they were wearing head to toe. Try doing the same for vehicles, houses, or any details inside a location.

Another fun exercise to build up your skills is to pause a TV cop show right before the traffic stop, call, or when they just engage. Use your inner vision to see what happens next, and then watch the show to see how close you were. You will find that if you preprogram some of the body signals, you will get a more complete account of what happens next. For instance, if the suspect flees the scene and you receive your signal for weapon and drugs, this gives a more accurate account of what is going to occur and why, and how it's going to happen.

If you receive visual information as flashes or short video clips, you can recall more from your visions with the assistance of your Higher Guidance. Ask to have your vision replayed. I ask my Higher Guidance to replay the vision and make it brighter so I can see. I ask that important details be highlighted. At times I ask for action to be slowed down. Much of your psychic gift can be adjusted this way. There will be times when the Higher Guidance lets you know that it can't be changed, so that is just the way it will be in that case. You have to trust this and know that you are not doing something wrong. There are some things we are just not allowed to know.

Reading a Suspect's Energy

A suspect can be anyone who committed a crime or is suspected of committing a crime. Don't assume that it is the most obvious person. In order to read clearly, try reading without knowing which suspect you are reading. For instance, if law enforcement has three suspects, have them be identified to you just as individuals 1, 2, 3 and so on.

Start with individual 1. Allow the information to come in naturally without trying to figure out what it means. Say it out loud or write it down to read to the investigator. Notice body signals and vibrations, visions, or smells that come to you. Be detailed with your description of any people you see. Here is a good way to organize what you are seeing:

Sex
Race
Age
Height

Weight
Build (thin, stocky, etc.)
Scars, Marks, Tattoos (stretch to get exact location on body and any other information that comes in with that)
Facial hair
Clothing (from head to toe description, e.g., blue baseball cap, white shirt, blue jeans, unknown shoes)
Name (include nickname)
Address (detailed as you can)
Mental state
Gang affiliation
Vehicle information (color, make, model, 2 dr, 4 dr, convertible, distinguishing marks, stickers, damage, license plate number and state, and any other information)
Their connection to this case
Check maps for any evidence, locations for offense
Evidence that has not been located (specify what it is and where it is located)
Anyone assisting this suspect in the crime (detailed using this list again for each person)
Allow general information regarding the case to come through.

Allow the investigator to ask questions if they have them. Always stay grounded and centered during this because it is easy for them to go to the information they believe is the answer instead of what the answer actually is.

Reading by Holding Evidence

If you are going to hold evidence, you will need to isolate your reading of the evidence from:

- evidential information related to the previous owners and people who have connected with this piece of evidence.
- the investigator's goals and ideas.
- any previous beliefs you have about this type of crime or this particular case.
- any stressors you have related to being wrong or miscommunications.

Remain professional at all times if you wish to be called upon again. Even if you are seeing awful things in your mind's eye, you need to appear calm and centered to the investigator—no drama or psychic talk about demons, psychic attack, entities, etc. When reading an item from a violent offense, remember to:

- receive just the information you need to and don't take it in.
- stay centered and calm so that you don't scare the investigator.
- give concise facts and details with professionalism and not your ego.
- remain objective and do not become emotionally involved. (Save crying or drama of any kind until after you leave because it is essential for you to clear this after the reading if you are holding it.)

Always respect the rules of evidence. Understand that the bag is as close as you will get to the item, and you can get clear information through the bag. In rare situations, if the item is not in a bag, you must wear gloves. Remember to clear your energy before holding any additional items. The investigators won't give you validation in most cases because they would be going against department policies and procedures by telling you things about an ongoing investigation. Accept this and move on.

These cases can be extremely hard if the case touches something that hits close to home for you. This means you may have to re-center yourself in order to read for the case assigned and not your own experience that is unresolved.

What to Do at an Outdoor Scene before Reading Energy

There are certain demonic entities that like to create distractions and chaos. In the case of outdoor scenes of missing persons or other cold cases, you will have these entities trying to distract you and take energy so that you can't continue your work. A specific Earth demon will attempt this. This entity is Fierro. In a course on Demonology, I learned the name of this entity and asked my Higher Guidance for a prayer and more information to use before reading outdoor scenes.

Remove Interfering Demonic Entity (Fierro)

The character of this demonic entity is of distraction and torment. It is a very low-ranking demon cast out even by the demonic realm. The only thing this entity can do, in our time period, is manipulate nature to cause disruption for humans whose Souls are not clear of wants and needs or who have greed or chaos in their lives. At an investigation scene, these people might be deterred by biting insects, flooded areas, branches falling, or a feeling that they need to leave.

Fierro can create imbalances in nature and create spiritual blocks for many. It creates attachments with the individual, which cause disturbances in sleep, meditation, sex, and any spiritual work. This demon has knowledge from both darkness and light and uses it to create a bond with greed. It hides buried treasure and makes it impossible for anyone to find lost or stolen things. It makes sure the secrets buried within the Earth stay secrets.

To remove or clear from a person or land, use the following prayer. The process of clearing after this prayer can take from ten minutes to forty minutes to start creating a clearer space to read. Plan accordingly. It is better to do the prayer at the location if possible.

> **I ask almighty God to preserve and protect all Earth spirits, humans, plants, animals, insects, and other life forms of God's pure creation from this Fierro. I transform the darkness into eternal Light and restore grace in every cell structure or Soul in the Universe. I ask for the power of God to transform all negative entities associated with the Fierro to the Divine bright state they started as and to create a change for positive environmental beliefs from the Souls of all.**
>
> **Expel Fierro to the pits of Hell, binding him there until he is released from the demonic enslavement he chose to have in Satan's jail, eternal until the end of his existence or until he turns to the original Source of Light and Divine oneness. Amen**

Consider Spiritual and Physical Safety

Taking your physical safety into account is a must in reading these cases. It is not a game to see what you can do. Definitely do not read alone in these places as you will not be grounded in a place you can't control. In your own sacred space is much different than being on site. I often have my armed police officer husband with me so that I can focus on reading and not on who is walking around, or if a suspect is near. If it's not safe or legal to go to the outdoor scene, don't do it.

Discern Energies

Energy signatures are energetic blueprints of tragic or emotional events still on the scene where they occurred. It is just energy, so you can't interact with it. You can receive a complete account of what happened without details of time, date, or names unless they were spoken there. You will have to speak to your Higher Guidance, Earth Spirits, the victim, or other spiritual energy connections to get more information. Some pieces of information might be conflicting when you read for the cases. It does not mean they are incorrect, just that different perspectives may be seen.

Many energy signatures can be at the same location, which will take some navigating, but it is possible. With your intent, isolate the date and time if you know it prior to reading. Use a digital recording of your findings because you may be at a higher vibration and not grounded as much as usual, which could cause you to not retain information for as long. Working with a partner who can record and ground you when necessary is essential. You will have to navigate the energy of crimes and negative events. Having a partner there will allow for grounding in fearful energy. They can remind you that you are safe, your family is safe, and they are watching the scene while you work. Both people can't read and help each other. One should hold the energy until the other is done, and then they can switch. Each person's gift is different, so you may gain more information when multiple people read the case. It is not necessary, but if you work in groups, it is an interesting result.

You may pick up objects you are guided to or lie on the ground for the reading. Go with what your Higher Guidance is telling you at the time. Each case is different. However, if you find evidence on a scene do not touch it. Mark it without disturbing it. Contact a law enforcement officer to do any further removal or checking of a scene. It is possible you may revisit a scene and find something left behind by the original investigators. Just report it if you are not sure.

Allow yourself to connect with the Earth Spirits and ask about the case. Also try connecting with the missing person to get any information they can add. However, some victims do not want to be found and may interfere or lie to you.

An additional complication with traumatic events on location is that an energetic tear in the Universe may have occurred, creating a leak of energy either into or out of the scene. You might feel this energy under the right side of your rib cage or see it as a dark purple pulsating light. Allow yourself to heal the tear while you are there by directing your healing energy to seal the space.

What to Do When Your Personal Hurts and Traumas Interfere with Reading for a Case

Pings are areas of imbalance inside our own energy. When we work with energy, these areas may get triggered if the work we are doing has similarities with areas we are still healing within ourselves. These areas of imbalance can originate in any direction of time. They are always located in the Root Chakra and cause a feeling of fear or uncertainty. To continue working:

1. First acknowledge the energy and place it in a separate space (above your head) to be handled at a later time.
2. Plug yourself back into the Earth and to God/Source/Creator
3. Center yourself and continue

How to Clear the Ping

1. First plug yourself back in and center
2. Allow yourself to sit in the energy to observe
3. Locate the first time you felt this way
4. It will feel like it is real and at the moment or origin
5. Mirror and Freeze
6. Give it to God/Source/Creator
7. Replace the energy you removed with positive, e.g. unconditional love, peace, courage.

Mirroring allows you to isolate the energy. "Mirror and Freeze" keeps stubborn energy isolated (Ego) if mirroring alone does not work. Your thought forms are very powerful and will read as true energy if you don't remove them. Have a way to breathe and take a break from the energy. One option is to imagine a creative space in which to breathe and be protected and free of distraction. Sit there until you are ready to continue or stop the reading if necessary.

Make a chart of the following terms, and use Eye Tracking or a pendulum as guided to help you navigate the energy:

Lower Your Thought Form	Mirror Thought Form
Mirror Ego	Listen
Believe You Are Getting Correct Information	Mirror Your Judgments
Lower Your Expectations	Hold Limonite
Lower Your Instinct	Free Your Energy
Imagine a Creative Space to Read	Mirror the Energy

<u>Energy that Can Interfere with a Clear Reading</u>

If fear is blocking you, refer back to the "Removing Fear Steps" on pages 9 and 10. To see if any of the following outside energies are affecting the clarity of your reading, you can check with your Higher Guidance (a pendulum can be used):

Lower Vibration Energy – Putting both Dolomite Marble on your left side at waist level and Black Tourmaline on your right side at waist level is calming and allows you to work in areas of low vibration and separates the power from the Heart Chakra.

Blocking Thought Forms
Victim
Deceptive/Leading Energy
Connecting Energy that may allow for incorrect reading of cases
Twin or Multiple births
Family Ties
Love Interest
Powerful Trauma
Lost Loved One
Imprinting
Tempting Death

Step-by-Step Reading of an Unsolved Case

Determine the target energy you will be reading.

Is the energy in your highest good to work with? You may have to walk away, and that is OK.

Read your own energy in response to the targeted energy.

List your "ping" areas to be worked on at later time.

Isolate your energy from the targeted energy.

Mirror the targeted energy to isolate.

See if there are attachments to the targeted energy.

Remove attachments. (Call in Archangel Michael.)

Mirror your Ego.

Imagine a Creative Space to read in. (Saying the words "Creative Space" connects you to an isolated chamber without distractions.) Listen.

Common Sense in Not Harming Victim Families

All missing persons cases should be investigated by police and family as if the person is still alive. You will miss pertinent details if you assume death. Places and witnesses will never be checked if they do not believe the person is still alive. Never harm a victim's family by telling them you think the loved one who is missing is dead. You can tell the police that if you wish but never the family. Also, do not share graphic details with them because they will never be able to forget them. These are real people, and this is not a game.

Thank you for being focused on purpose with the intent to help, even if that means you can't get information for a person. Don't tell them what they already know. Reach higher with God to bring in things people have forgotten, individuals to talk to again, evidence not yet located, a fresh perspective outside the case, or locations and detailed information that would be of benefit.

PART 2

The object of not wanting something will create an experience of regret. We often choose not to do things that would bring us joy in order to avoid the feeling of inadequacy that often follows. The result of not wanting something will create an experience of regret. We follow the path of the least apparent resistance so that we do not have to experience joy and then loss. The path of least resistance creates a knowing of future benefits that are unseen to the naked eye. A connection to All That Is and Will Always Be is the path of least resistance. When this happens you are aware that you are not changing a thing, and this regret can be felt in your Soul and the Soul of the others around you, related to you, looking up to you, and co-creating with you. I can co-create with you if you can put in the work to better yourselves and the others around you. This work comes with a price. Peace.

Can You Lift Your Fellow Man to a Level That Outweighs Your Resistance to Change?

More times than not, you create change without creating resistance for yourself. This change moves you to better financial security, your dream house, and other Earthly desires, but it does not include the purpose that God has assigned for you here. You must move deeper into your Soul, your spirit, and believe that there is a way to belong in the higher realms. We create dreams within ourselves without including the reason for our existence. These beliefs continue to make us feel lonely, afraid, indifferent, and unfulfilled. The only way you can accomplish what you chose to come to this planet to accomplish is by being direct. Say it like it is. Create like it is. Dream like it is. We allow our respect for one another to defeat our reason for coming here. Our ignorance about our fellow man does not allow the growth of man, or ourselves, because we believe we are already being true to ourselves.

In this world, you have created an alternate reality that is your own. When you add that to several million others, it creates no change. Distance between you and God is created without even realizing it. We feel we must fit in and keep others at peace. Are we really keeping others at peace? I think not. Even when we are alone, we can't find the peace we are looking for. I ask my brothers to change their way of thinking, to connect the dots and create peace for themselves and others. It has been known to cause resistance when you create an alternate reality, a truth that is not aligned with the actual truth but one's own illusion. Illusion remains illusion and never fully connects with the energy of change because it is separate.

You may wake up from the dream feeling it was real, but after a few minutes you are right back where you started and who you were before. This is what illusion is. I have a clean house, I have clean children, I have lots of money....illusion. The emptiness of this creation is paralyzing to those who create it. To stay within this thought form and keep this illusion alive requires great strength and countless hours of preparations. You keep going around and around, never stepping out for fresh air, stopping only to rest for a short while before starting this ongoing process again and again. This is when you start to look outside yourself for a way to self-medicate to bring peace within: alcohol, drugs, indiscretions, food, and any other way to numb this pain inside.

We even try to blame others for the inadequacy we feel, pulling them into our emptiness. When that does not work, we find ways to create false realities and belief systems to take our minds off the task at hand: a new job, friend, house, or car to bring the mind away from the internal torment and misery from within. We may even try to get others to feel sorry for us and what we have created for ourselves. That's right. We have created this for ourselves. The ownership belongs to us—all of us, not just you. Maybe the love you lost becomes the way you first realize why you are here and what your purpose is.

I am Metatron of God, a supreme creator of love and spirit into the newness of All That Is. I am the belief in the Creator of our lives and the lives of others, a belief that started at the steps of Heaven. I am a kind, loving Soul that works closely with God to accomplish a Divine order of faith beyond what the eye can see, beyond the love you think is the highest. I travel to many realms in order to create a peaceful, honest paradigm, which may be felt in the heart of all men. I am a supporter of the troops of Angelic beings that work across this Universe and beyond this reality. I love all, and I support all alignment of God on every level. I am not only an Archangel but a co-creator within God's Divine plan instituted with orders to divide fact from fiction and to destroy the alternative to love and peace, which is hate, greed, and war. The opinions of others do not affect my mission. Our journey together creates peace in alignment with the Creator of All That Is Was and Will Always Be. I don't have to be afraid because I know the truth of your existence and what is meant to be. I believe. Do you?

All creatures love on some level. Love is direct and not complicated. It just is. Love is peace brought to you by seeing yourself looking beyond yourself to connect with another living creature and realizing how you fit in God's plan. Love is moving over and letting God breathe through you for the benefit of another. Peace within occurs when you can accomplish that undivided, completely surrendered love for another. It is when you step outside yourself and connect with God to bring that light through unobstructed, undivided, none withheld. Bring it through as though you are not even there or changing it. Where there is love there is no fear. Fear is baseless when it is paired with love. Fear is a barrier to love and one's own truth. Fear creates chaos on all levels of mankind.

There are so many ways love can be extinguished. Even the trees will fall one day. Enough has been said to create a paradigm of eternal peace and wellness. Creating change without fault, even truth will only create a space of a new reality. Plug into the current paradigm and start there. Those indignant to the truth of God have created a large open spectrum of truth. False prophets have always roamed the Earth spreading a fear-based reality of God and truth only for the wicked. In a fear-based society, these false prophets rule with those entrusted to uphold the false words and ideals. They are safer here than the real prophets because they have a circle of fear-based trust, creating fear at the thought of speaking against them. God did not choose the ones of untruth, fear, and upheaval. God chose you to speak against them to spread words of faith, love, and trust of the Divine love we all have inside us.

A Message from Archangel Gabriel

This begins the second part of our journey: believing that all you need is within your connection to All That Is and being able to navigate safely and lovingly through life with this connection. Begin by watching the reaction that others have to power and truth, as they have been waiting for you to speak this truth. This truth sparks the power within them to be able to clearly see the storms in front of them. When they see from this perspective, the illusion disappears and creates a grand opening of their connection to God/Source/All That Is energy. Once tapping into this part of yourselves, you will be unstoppable in your courage and dignity in presenting the truth. There is not fear in this place, and it links you directly into your spiritual destiny.

The Bible in the Heart of All Men

When we read the *Bible*, there are so many verses filled with knowledge and truth on varying topics. It is about love, truth, God, creation, indignity, evil, unworthiness, fame, and fortune. Each scripture represents a part of the truth about all of eternity, of grace, and of understanding the Divine higher purpose of man and his knowledge here on Earth. It tells how to grow without harming others and how to have without taking from others. It contains the evolution of the human psyche. The *Bible* paraphrases the energy of Divine love sent here from God/Creator/Universe and All That Is, Will Be, and Will Forever Remain in the hearts of man, the Soul, the gratitude of an experience with the Holy Creator and keeper of time. Fault is not of this God realm but of man. When you write from the Holy Grail of All That Is, when you share the secrets of the Holy Grail, the *Bible* is born. Historically, Jehovah was the Creator of all. Hold the chalice and experience your own Divine intervention as it is already within you.

The following verses come from Divine inspiration of the paraphrasing of Jesus the Christ, giving his depiction in modern terms and language approved by the Holy Creator, sealed with love and hope for brighter change and growth, through his own eyes while holding the chalice. Let him be your guide in determining another avenue of verse from him and not from a collection of writers. This author has been given Divine truth as she is of the realm of record keeping and paradigm shifts in all directions of this Earth and beyond. Her truth is of men and this paradigm, connecting through the higher realms to establish change and witness the truths of man. Will you encourage her to keep this paradigm going with more secrets of the Holy Grail, the chalice of truth also termed the Arc of the Covenant? Within the realm of non-existence, there is a Grail and Arc available to all without the necessity of war and change. Deep there within your Holy Existence we instill a variety of deeply buried secrets of this realm and of the distance of our God/Creator and His path beyond the imagination of man.

Each man is born with this knowledge accessible—that wonder you are born with, the childlike knowledge of more than this existence. However, truths can dissipate when you throw your entirety into human existence. Karma can also keep you from your connection to this truth if you have not acted favorably, but that too can be healed in time and with work on furthering human paradigms in a more positive direction. Will you take the time to see what wonders lie dormant within your Soul, life path, and truth?

To bring this writing to you, I must first go within my Soul body. I breathe and ask the Divine Holy Creator that I may come out of the dormant state and into the human consciousness, much like Noah. I will then surrender my ideals, concerns, skepticism, fears, greed, anger, resistance, evil, and replace it with the knowing that comes from believing that somewhere out there is another place I know that cannot be taken or destroyed. With every cell and part of this Earthly body and beyond—in all parts of my existence in all directions of time and space and in all realities, realms, spirit, God—I remember this place in which I am a Divine Creator and a perpetuator of truth, justice, divinity, Divine love, Karma, faith, and trust in our holy existence.

In front of me I see the Arc of the Covenant, a beautiful representation of All That Is and Will Ever Be. I hold my truth, knowing that when it is activated by the forces of God and the Divine, only truth can remain present. The opening of this Arc can only be done with God's will and approval. When it opens, a modern example of truth will appear along with the knowing that is needed to understand the symbol, voice, command, or teaching. O Holy Creator, so that I may serve with absolute trust and faith, I ask you now to open the Arc for us to see the truth once buried within.

It is open. What do you see, hear, smell, acknowledge, or know? Does it take you to a place, show you a symbol, or stop Karma you do not need? So many things are possible with this knowledge. The secret is that it cannot be used to harm. That is impossible. Any intent to harm will never allow you to access these Divine truths. You must be of Divine faith and love.

The Arc of the Covenant remains eternally buried inside this Earth until a future time when those who are here can handle its contents. This device contains knowledge of lost worlds and the demise of many races of human beings and animals that once roamed the Earth. If this were to be found at the present time, its contents would be destroyed in a power struggle between good and evil. For now this device is safely buried at sea and will be accessible by the Soul Mind only through extensive dedication to the truth.

Being your truth alone is a reason to seek it. Know that your Soul contains secrets of this time and others. We may ask God to instill the knowledge of our existence, but human barriers can control the mind and distort this truth. The mind, by nature, allows you to see and hear what you want. This is always easier. The barriers of the human mind must be altered and removed in order to be able to connect, gather, and retain the authentic truths that await you. If you are lucky enough to have God connect and open the Arc, you will see truth whether you are ready to see it or not. The force of this energy does not allow anything but truth, integrity, and peace to remain.

Divine paraphrasing of Jesus relating to the following verses, hymns, prayers, and beliefs in this Holy Grail of All That Is and Will Ever Be has been given to this author to share. When reading this section, allow yourself to receive from this energy, as well, to see where it takes you.

John 7:38

He who believes in me, out of his heart will flow rivers of living water. I could feel the words of the Lord coming to me like waves. The more I believed the more I could share with the world. The love is so strong, and it goes into every dark place. It makes it bright. It heals.

Be Still and Know

I feel you with, my Lord. I can pretend that you are not with me. I can hurt inside, or you can challenge me to grow. The isolation I feel is not of this world but of knowing of you and being separate. Join with me, my Lord, so I may grow.

Jesus Loves Me This I Know

This love, this guidance will deliver me from my sins, the sins of my brother and All That Is. Balance creates this within me, my balance. I stand before you, O Lord. I repent, and I choose your light. Please, Lord, have me.

The Lord's Prayer

Everything you have ever dreamed of you already possess. This light, love, dedication is inside you. Choose to ask for help this way, and I connect to you the knowledge and love you deserve. Isolate not, dear one, as you are here beside me. Each passing moment brings you back to this knowing. Be not of the storms but of the light. Ask and I give to you my world, my blessing, and my unconditional love, as each should be without strings or limits. Grant me this wish, O Lord, as I am your faithful servant. I love you.

Hail Mary

I adore. Please lift me, dear Mother. I ask for your forgiveness and strength when I am weak, when I am strong, when I am lost or forgotten. Please heal me, dear Mother. The loss of my child leaves me weak. Where are you, dear Mother?

When I touch your Soul, you know I am here. Many years have passed since we met. I can't describe Heaven to you in one word. Forgive all, love all, create all. Each time we cross paths, you feel me connect with your Soul. The light comes through in your eyelids. We join each other not of this plane but of God's plane, divided by nothing but love. Can you feel me there beside you? Are you afraid? Christ is here beside you. We can bring you forgiveness, but you must take it inside you. This light of forgiveness is beyond the spectrum of color. You endure, dear child. Let me help you. By the grace of forgiveness, you are blessed with this Divine light, and peace lives within you, dear child. Fear not. You are blessed.

I kneel beside you. I see your thread. Can you forgive me, dear Mother? Where did I go wrong? I escaped to the freest place I could find beneath this Earth. Will I ever be free? I am afraid because I have sinned against God. I decided to.

Psalm 23

In the beginning there was chaos that turned into light—love, determination to achieve, and so much more. I ask of you to remember three things: to believe you and God are of equal place, to love beyond your mask of illusion, to bring the truth to others of the Divine mission of love, guidance, peace, charity and love. Between worlds we find the illusion that distracts from the true purpose of man. We agree to disagree with others. Between worlds, God is a part of your Divine mission and plan. Call to him when you have weakened to the world you are currently in. Expect the miracles of this love to respond no matter where you are. This love is beyond your voice and knowledge. Peace within the kindness of man will free you all. Beyond this world and others, you make the love ripple to others of all types and beings. All of them feel the love equally beyond measure. Amen.

Psalm 23:6

I crossed paths with the Lord on my way to Bethlehem. He stood by me and gave me courage and strength. He asked me to bear witness to this miracle child. I left them right before they made it to town. I canceled my plans to remain witness, but the miracle was of such a magnitude I could not breathe. The determined carried on even knowing how tough this road would be. Alone among the men of this place, riddled with terrible pains and wars, why bring this to me?

Alone in a chamber I started to scribe the events that had just occurred, knowing there would be a penalty if I were found. Alone at last to create the document that will remain in the hearts of those who read it. Penance is steep in this world. I create and achieve but suffer at the hand of man that does not understand me, my mission, and my love for our Lord. Please don't banish me from Heaven if I do not finish this task. It is beyond the world I know, but I remember you, O Lord. Bring me peace so that I may move forward. My strength is with you, my Lord. Banish me not as I am true to man.

Genesis

All thee who cherish the shepherd will not be left to fend for themselves. I tried to lift the innocence of man to higher levels, but the exchange left me no choice other than to recreate the world again—starting from scratch to try again, to evolve, to grow. Those who were left behind had no business trying to restrain me, my life, my journey, my God. I can only explain what you are willing to hear. Evolving means that you cherish what you have loved and move forward from that space. What part of that does not make sense? Even the human mind is free to roam. Roam with me, not against me. I try countless hours to recreate this. I am tired. The explosion of the infinite universe is that which you will never be able to repay. Countless hours of creation that move the paradigm from here to there. What is this? I need to grow, develop, nurture and co-create. What happened? How did I get here? Where are we going next?

Genesis 39

About thirty thousand years ago, man was without faith, which is a needed necessity to develop the human psyche.

Genesis 41

The Shepherd cannot wait until the sheep are gone. He must wait there alone. Only the truth of the realms of the universe will create chaos. Be not afraid. Experience my spirit, my realm, my truth, as it shall be known to you.

Genesis 41:14-25

A man is a journey even unto himself. Fear of the wrath will always create change. I wish to make this your mission, your belief, your destiny. Not mine.

Proverbs 10

I'm not often alone with spirit. I can talk with the Lord. I can exchange the gifts of spirit—the give and take of being a Christian. I am at peace. I have Egyptian roots and can access them through spirit when I am tired or hungry. The place in my Soul that needs nourishment is fed by the Lord.

Proverbs 10:11

I will remain a faithful servant of the Lord, regardless of what you say to me. I remain a calm and fractured servant of the Lord. I only acknowledge that of light. I only acknowledge the destiny of my Soul and my Soul's Soul. Our Father's Soul belongs to us all. Stop treating the persecuted with injustice. In Jesus name I forgive all of you for this injustice and this eternal pain you have caused me.

Proverbs 10:12

I am enough as I told you. I have fears but am not beneath you, my Lord. I am alone and afraid. I thought about you a hundred times. Belonging to you and what that means, there is only peace in my heart. I can arrange to be with you soon, my Lord. I can breathe the light of your Soul. I can envision your face here with me. I want to be free.

Proverbs 10:14

I will wait here with my candle lit. I know you will find me soon. I am ready. I think that you may be in front of me. I can recall when the last memory was spoken. The smallest dream can connect the order of change. The depth of life remains in the dignity of the Soul.

I can't change the dignity of others as they are without patience. I can dream of this and connect this and wait. I would like a chance to redirect your Soul to a place of patience and belief in a higher power, positive thoughts, dreams and affirmations, but you will not let me bring this forward to you. I think the stars were born before, and the dream of power within only ignites more stars. As many stars as you dream will grow. Lessons will bring you to another layer of these stars since they are infinite. A coordinator of the stars we call you. The destiny of one will move you past the resistance you feel. Push forward, dear, to create the highest level of activation stars that you can. You must reach a higher plane to eliminate resistance. Resistance is cheap, so everyone has it. I want you to dream, dream of higher stars.

Samuel 2:22

I am but afraid of the demons within. I deny none as I pass through this land. I created a path of stars. I collect the Souls of the wicked and connect them to the stars. When they move past them, they are reborn in light. This light reflects out into the universe creating an arc of light. The bend is in such a manner that it creates a prism of enlightened space divided into none. I can be lightened by my path of stars. I can dream of life within the stars of stars. The space in my Soul that creates everlasting joy touches my Crown Chakra and breathes life into the dark. The dark is isolated fragments of the creature they originated from. The choice to create this darkness is not of God but of man.

Ruth 3:14

The files of Jesus have left out this person as sacred. There is much harm done when the writing is of the writer and not of the Lord. They are of the Lord but not devoted to scripture and are not created equal.

Psalm 19

The meaning of bread in the Hebrew Bible is not as simple as you may think. There is scripture from thousands of years ago disputing this claim. Buried beneath the sea are scriptures of faith thrown overboard when the spirit was alone. Calm rivers and storms—the dearest ones to us are the storms to enlightenment. The boring, stationary fear of being alone is of the highest illusion. Expanding peace within the storm of enlightenment is true faith, as is being in spirit while opening the door for your son to do the same. Imagine the results of this knowing. Creating obstacles only changes your plan for peace and clarity.

Psalm 22

Peace be with you, adorn you, cover you. Wings. Wings of light and orange petals. Beneath the trees swollen with fruit, crying beneath, tortured Soul, peace beneath, cry alone. Why? Beneath this cherished realm will be peace. My peace is your peace even in trying times. O please, beneath me peace. A challenge of youth is more of a goal of choice. A bearer of truth that tames the beast, shapes his mind, creates his Soul. Miraculous beings of light, all gold and orange with defined petals. Peace beneath. My O Lord, I am new to this realm. I cry to you beneath the peace. I am well. I am lost. I needed to be lost.

Psalm 30

The only joy to the wicked is faith. Faith fallen without joy. Born again to defend against the wickedness. I trust the Earth will give me guidance. I can entangle these trees of light beyond my means. I can catch the glory of the Lord beneath these trees. I pray to you, Lord, as you have sent me beyond my means.

Psalm 43

I ask for your opinion, dear Lord. I can't find the way to your kingdom. I've lost my way. I need you. Can you see my storm in front of me? Can you see why it pains me so? I wish to see your face at the end of it all. If the storm threatens the peace of the kingdom, will it fall? Is there truth in this discovery? Can we claim victory today?

Psalm 45

In Egypt man has created a life worth living. If you have fame you do not belong here. There are many ways to slay a dragon, and this is not the means to an end. Your futile efforts to move the Divine out of this land will not bring peace but discourse. The way of the land does not support this means.

Psalm 41

Hungry are those who are weak. The time has come for the lonely to become strong. Are you able to create a love of God to pass on to your children? Before long they will be grown. Create dreams to share with the children of God. Be at peace.

John 15

I proclaim the truth cannot be obtained from your Soul without reason. The reason you are here is not of stone but of God. I want you to find the truth within all; be that truth; and always remember who you are.

Psalm 128

In the forces of evil, one will never be entrapped by another unless they choose to. Evil is not able to remove your will. Forces of evil have no reign over you. All of you are covered by Divine sovereignty. Each is to his own path of alignment, not to be interfered with unless you choose to be interfered with. The Lord will make you his priority when you allow the evil not to be part of you.

Psalm 124

I am tired of feeling the breeze when I am cold. I am tired of the places You touch that are not in alignment with my Soul. I choose peace. This is no longer my journey, and with You I will have peace.

The Divine does not conquer your will. Do not let the faith of others determine your will. If you feel free, then so be it. If you feel that you are on a more dignified path than others, so be it. Do not be afraid that you will be forgotten, as moving forward often comes with change. Some will leave and some will prosper with you. That is not a reason to quit this journey. It is a reason to continue. Continue as a free spirit, determined by your will and alignment with the Holy Creator. In Jesus name you are free, and so it is.

Did you know that faith can conquer all? It is the strongest connection you will ever feel. Create a space of love in your heart to release any hidden corded energies to your Soul. Do not fear this as it will free your time and energy to concentrate on the task at hand. Even with the purest energy field, there is always a layer of new growth that can open old doors. Ask that the Divine Creator close these doors permanently so that you can grow without having to revisit these old wounds time and time again. The Divine Source can correct this if you pray for this help and guidance:

> **Dear Lord, please bless all those around me with your Divine love and guidance. Create a place to properly disconnect these corded energies without major effort and pain.**

Beneath the realms of the Divine are lost love and people. I cannot explain in detail how this came to light, but I can tell you it causes the Divine to feel pain of a human nature. It sends the frequency of loss of Divine faith to the holder of the truth of Mohammed. It is like a wavelength of Divine trust has been broken, and you lose faith. Even knowing this, you will understand that there is a break in the universe—a catastrophic break in the universal energy. Each time a law is broken when the holder is aware of the truth, they will feel or know of the severity of the indignation that is being allowed.

There may be times where a truth has more power by not being spoken. This is one of those cases. Speaking truth stops the speaker's path, and a choice has to be made whether it is better for the speaker to be silent in a specific situation. If it is God's will to have you keep silent, the truth that causes danger or the feeling of inadequacy must be altered to centered and at peace to continue the mission. "I limit the amount of truth" does not feel right to the Soul, which causes the Earthly body to feel anxious, insecure, or without mission for a period of time before and after a major event. Major events include catastrophic hatred, war, and collision between good and evil, and earthquakes caused by misuse of power to the Earth's land. Yes, you have people on your Earth using power that is creating an imbalance to the structure below your land, which causes an acceleration of catastrophic tornadoes and earthquakes. This mining and drilling is feeding the people, but it is causing damage beyond repair to the top layers of the Earth. Don't depend on the truths of the environment through just natural realms. You are creating chaos on your own lands.

If you are ever to change the way you feel about the *Bible*, truths of the universe, faith, and your Divine oneness with Creator, you must value your own inner realm—your voice that tells you the difference between good and bad, faith and false prophet. The inner knowing is the direct link to your Soul's spinal cord of electrical Divine impulses that connect you to your higher knowledge. Start to believe that you are part of All That Is and have a way to change what needs to be changed or altered in order to assist in ascension in this realm and all those connected to it. If what you are sensing is that a tempered cell needs to be altered, healed, or renewed, you have all that you need both inside you and with your outer connection to the impulses that connect us all energetically, emotionally, spiritually—in all forms of our cells, our bodies, our voices, and our needs. Conflict within you will stop when you repeat:

This realm is never divided by race or war. It is never neglected by peace. It reigns over its own truth. It forces no one to leave. It delivers from evil means. Our Source remains within and ever present between. In Jesus' name. Amen.

Mark 8:34

I have created a dream. Out of the darkness flies a white dove full of grace and peace, one mere bird symbolizing the dreams of all men. It allows me to see the alternative, unheard truth. A happiness and a peace that is love created by me in this universe. I awaken to see that things are still the same, but a spark of light remains. It's a beginning of sorts. One flame of one person's truth created with a mere thought that lasts but a second. This creation magnifies itself and reaches out to the others with similar thoughts, connecting to a new consciousness created in spirit. Waves of gold light and branches of gold defy meaning, allowing a mass opening of consciousness. Dreams survive eternities in space and time, allowing the past to be reformed, transformed, and idealized. I am a maker of dreams and realities. Even the merest part of my Soul is impacted by this dreaming truth. Can I depend on others to restore my faith? I think not. I must find it within the space of my own consciousness. Equally debating the facts from my dreams, restoring my faith in its due time, I am an equally powerful creature. My need to restore truth and faith are mine and mine alone.

Hebrews 9

Undeveloped, underfed, debilitating allowances of greed, I scorn the truth of you who allows my demise. Asking to be enslaved, crying, unnatural death, why? I don't know why. Can't the part of the Universe that is weak be broken? I idolize the dream of the Lord, whose faith I do not understand. I can't depend on man, I must depend on you. Each day I live, I dream of your face. How will I survive this ordeal? Man is unkind. I can't break what is already broken. Twelve more days you say until my demise. How will I survive? I dream of your face, O Lord.

1 Corinthians 14

Until twelve years ago I left my country in a state of disrepair, not knowing what the future would bring. Undeniable faith leading my way, I dream visions of a new world. You and I are explaining the truth as it was intended. Parables of the Almighty are creating little sparks of joy in the children. Allowances are unlimited. I can't believe the possibility of what faith can bring. I expect that this will be the most amazing creation ever, if I can pull it off. My Creator summons me, asks me to deviate from the original plan. I am unsure as this is the faith I have grown to love. Immediate means of control cannot be exchanged with the demon spirits; this is not the faith I have grown to love. I must remain. This is my destiny, the way my Soul believes. I hear you, dear Lord, but I must remain.

A Channeled Writing from Jesus

Independent peace, meaning peace in you and not the others you serve, will leave you without breath. Independent truth, meaning truth that is you in a false place of self, will also leave you breathless. The challenge is to combine your wants and desires with the truth of God. Development of the Soul includes many lessons of peace within and outside the self. The self is not patient or kind without a Divine plan or mission. I asked that the eleventh day be spent in rest. The path to the Soul is dependent on your true desire and intention. Allowances enough to satisfy all that is needed and permitted are made before the Soul is at rest. Your future is independent of your spiritual desires to grow.

Calmness and truth rely on each other for balance. Small tasks and dreams are not satisfying unless the Soul agrees. Enough chaos will crumble any truth. Each dream depends on the next level of self-achievement and promotion. Even God has tasks and goals. No man is free of trials and tribulations. Promoting of sins is inexcusable. Violence will indeed be the fall of man.

The statue of me is not depicted in my true desire to be represented. I was afraid and then succumbed to injuries. The rendering is not true to the pain I knew inside and out. The fear I felt was astronomical compared to anything else I knew. When you see me lifted up to God, know it was God and not I that saved you. I am man, just like you, with a piece of Heaven inside my Soul. I love, desire, and dream just as you. I want just as you. I am eternally grateful for all God has chosen me to do and to share with you and the world.

I challenge you to lead a life that is grateful for all, even the little. Find love in ways you did not believe were possible, opening yourself to higher possibilities and strengths like God has taught me. I extend that gratefulness to you, as I know you want what I wanted: to make a difference in the world, which is lost and ungrateful, evil and loveless; to put a piece of Divine Heaven back where it has been lost for centuries; and to prevent the start of the fall. Only Angels with Divine powers and guidance can help reestablish this truth. We must say it time and time again: without one God we will never remain. I am my God's shepherd and will always bring truth in His name. The path of the Soul is not to be rewritten or destroyed by nameless disobedience or sheltered by the wants and desires of man on Earth. Most will be enlightened by truth, but some will hate beyond salvation. The measure of resistance relates directly to successes and true faith.

I asked my Lord for guidance during my pending death, and he told me of demons and destruction of man if the events did not happen. I chose peace instead of pain and was rewarded with eternal bliss in the chambers of Heaven and beyond. I am not better but secure in my faith and power to move the opposition, to bring in the peace of God and the love faith everlasting has taught me.

The most magical occurrence in my experience is when the children of God bring Divine lightness and spirit into the ordinary world. It amazes me every day. I need you to know I was afraid and that fear is OK if met with Divine faith. If we never feared, we would never grow. A new place brings fear; the unknown brings fear; love brings fear. Don't worry that you are not good enough because of fear. I ran and hid when I didn't know what to do. I pray. I shed tears. I feel love too much to bear. And I mourn. I need, and I return to faith. There is no way to defeat the world's evils without faith.

Chart of the Subconscious Mind

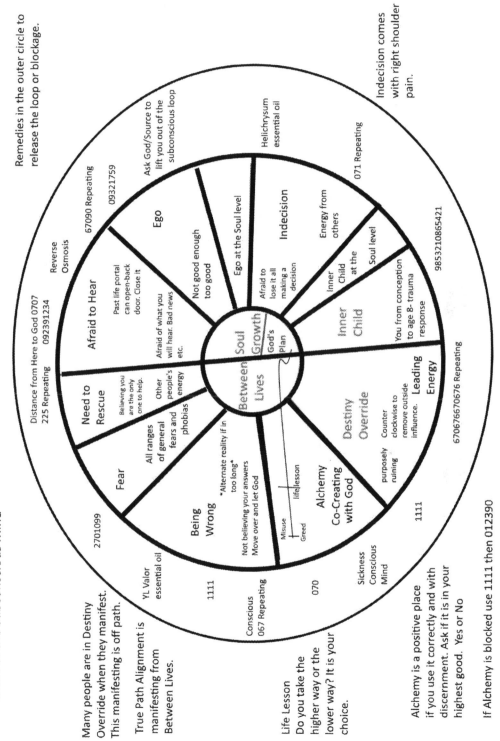

Remedies in the outer circle to release the loop or blockage.

Many people are in Destiny Override when they manifest. This manifesting is off path.

True Path Alignment is manifesting from Between Lives.

Life Lesson
Do you take the higher way or the lower way? It is your choice.

Alchemy is a positive place if you use it correctly and with discernment. Ask if it is in your highest good. Yes or No

If Alchemy is blocked use 1111 then 012390

Indecision comes with right shoulder pain.

Distance from Here to God 0707 225 Repeating

Reverse Osmosis

67090 Repeating

09391234

09321759

Ask God/Source to lift you out of the subconscious loop

Helichrysum essential oil

071 Repeating

985321085421

670676670676 Repeating

1111

070

2701099

YL Valor essential oil

1111

Conscious 067 Repeating

Sickness Conscious Mind

Ego

Afraid to Hear

Need to Rescue

Fear

Being Wrong

Alchemy Co-Creating with God

Destiny Override

Leading Energy

Inner Child

Indecision

Ego at the Soul level

Soul Growth

Between Lives

God's Plan

Not good enough too good

Past life portal can open-back door. Close it

Afraid of what you will hear. Bad news etc.

Believing you are the only one to help.

Other people's energy

All ranges of general fears and phobias

Alternate reality if in too long

Not believing your answers Move over and let God

Misuse Greed

life lesson

purposely ruining

Counter clockwise to remove outside influence.

You from conception to age 8- trauma response

Inner Child at the Soul level

Energy from others

Afraid to lose it all making a decision

Printed in the United States
By Bookmasters